Expectation
and Experience

A Joint Publication of
The American Academy of Religion
and Society of Biblical Literature

Volume 2
Expectation and Experience
by
Eugene V. Gallagher

Expectation _and_ Experience

Explaining Religious Conversion

Eugene V. Gallagher

Scholars Press
Atlanta, Georgia

Expectation and Experience

by
Eugene V. Gallagher

Library of Congress Cataloging in Publication Data

Gallagher, Eugene V.
　Expectation and experience : explaining religious conversion / by
　Eugene V. Gallagher.
　p. cm. -- (Ventures in religion ; no. 02)
　Includes bibliographical references.
　ISBN 1-55540-276-3 (alk. paper). -- ISBN 1-55540-537-1
　1. Conversion. 2. Converts--Psychology. 3. Experience (Religion)
I. Title. II. Series.
BL53.G34 1990
291.4'2--dc20
　　　　　　　　　　　　　　　　　　　　90-44590
　　　　　　　　　　　　　　　　　　　　CIP

Printed in the United States of America
on acid-free paper

Contents

Series Foreword

American culture broadly assumes that the term religion properly refers to a distinct domain of human behavior, thought, and experience. The American Constitution—which guarantees freedom of and from religion as a fundamental right—assumes religion as a given. Americans generally accept the idea that it is natural for people to have a religion and that being religious is a legitimate way to live.

Another way of putting this is to say that in American life religion is a native category. It is a basic classification that our culture routinely uses to sort out and organize the complexity of human existence. We conceive religion as an unquestioned aspect of human experience. It is an ordinary component of the way Western, and especially American, culture understands the world.

Because religion is a native category, we use it both abstractly and concretely. As an abstraction—much like the categories of "language" or "culture"—religion is a concept, a theoretical entity, that helps us to identify, label, and make sense of the discrete particulars of our own or other cultures. But, like all native categories, religion also claims to be concrete, self-evident, and inherently significant. Consequently, it is evocative but inarticulate. Our culture takes religion for granted as a meaningful and conventional trait of human being, but we grasp and employ religion intuitively more than we discern and deploy it discursively. We apprehend religion better than we comprehend it. As a culture, Americans seem to know that religion is important even when we cannot explain why. We think better *with* religion than we do *about* it.

The givenness of religion in American culture explains why it is important for Americans to study religion at some point in their education. To be sure, studying religion provides an interesting entry into the lives and cultures of other people. But, equally important, the study of religion gives us some needed perspective on ourselves by helping us question what is most familiar to us—our own native categories, the cultural lenses through which we see the world.

Ventures in Religion was created with just these issues in mind. It is a series of teaching books designed to spell out, for students across a wide institutional and educational spectrum, the issues of description, analysis, and interpretation that predominate in the study of religion. The series does not provide general introductions to discrete religions or to particular religious texts or artifacts. Rather, its volumes examine persisting questions, problems, concepts, and categories that have preoccupied the study of religion and helped to constitute it as a separate field of inquiry.

The series aims to show how the study of religion formulates and solves problems, how it shapes and directs intellectual curiosity. Thus, each volume focuses on what students of religion ask and how we ask it, on what we think and why we think it, and on why our questions and answers matter. The series attempts to address both the "What?" and the "So What?" of the study of religion.

Although volumes in the series supply basic information students need, they are neither conventional textbooks nor extended encyclopedia articles. Rather, each is written as an argumentative essay—a sustained statement of reasoned opinion and judgment—that encourages readers to think critically and to take a position. Books in this series are meant to be argued with and argued about. To that end, they are books readers should feel free to write in, with space on each page to do just that.

Because the volumes of *Ventures in Religion* are problem-centered or topic-centered, they can be used, singly or together, to complement the standard textbooks in religion, which often focus on specific traditions or texts. The editors hope that the series as a whole will be sufficiently flexible to respond to the varied interests and emphases of a wide range of instructional and institutional contexts.

Ventures in Religion is the first series jointly sponsored by the *American Academy of Religion* and the *Society of Biblical Literature* designed specifically for classroom use. As such, it signals a recognition by both learned societies of the importance of teaching in the intellectual life of the field. Indeed, the series may be understood as an acknowledgment that the future of the study of religion depends on the mutual stimulation and reinforcement of good scholarship and good teaching.

William Scott Green
University of Rochester

Preface

Scholarly writing in the study of religion frequently addresses questions about the definition of the field and its proper methods of study. In a small department of Religion at a small liberal arts college such questions take on a distinctly practical edge. When students are not specifically required to study religion as part of their general education or distribution requirements, it becomes all the more important to be able to present to them a clear vision of what they might be able to learn by investigating some of the forms of human religious life. When any course that a student takes in the study of religion is most likely to be that student's *only* course in the field, it becomes important to make sure that general questions about religion are addressed through the study of the particular subject matter of the course at hand, whatever it might be. Teaching about religion involves making scores of small decisions that implicitly and cumulatively define the field, its important questions, and the methods that most likely will produce interesting and persuasive answers.

Jonathan Z. Smith has argued that "for a student of religion . . . choice is everything."[1] That is at least as true of classroom as it is of the scholar's study— probably more so. Through the choice of courses to be offered, the inclusion of some but not other material in a given course, the focus of class presentations and discussions, the design of tests, papers, and other assignments—through choosing what to talk about and how to talk about it—instructors and departments of Religion contribute daily to the definition of the field.

My own sense of what the study of religion entails has been shaped by my continuing education over the past dozen years in the department of Religious Studies at Connecticut College. Through informal conversations with colleagues, planning and teaching courses together, and formal presentations and careful reading of each other's work, we have addressed the questions at the center of our field. As is appropriate at a small liberal arts college, I have spent much of my time trying to communicate to students some sense of the fascination that the study of human religious life can hold. I am convinced that anyone who so desires can learn interesting, significant, and even helpful, things about human life through the study of religion. It all depends, as so many things do, on how the subject is approached.

This book grows out of the thinking that I have done about religion with my students and colleagues at Connecticut College. Both groups have contributed to this book in various ways. For the past twelve years Garrett Green and Frank Johnson have been models of collegiality. Garrett Green's reading of this book in manuscript saved me from many errors and infelicities of expression; he has been particularly helpful in guiding me through the thickets of contemporary theology and philosophy of religion. I can only hope to return the favor in some way. Lindsey Harlan has also read the manuscript with a keen eye for sloppy prose and the sloppy thinking that it indicates. Many students have heard unawares parts of this book; they have rarely hesitated to tell me when something did not make sense and they have almost always been right. Joanne Maguire, my former student and, I hope, future colleague, has read the entire manuscript and contributed in many ways to its clarity.

During my final stages of work on this book I have benefitted from Jonathan Z. Smith's careful reading of the entire manuscript. Also, from the conception of this project to its completion William Scott Green, as editor of the Ventures in Religion series, has served as a sure and helpful guide.

The research for this book has been generously supported by Connecticut College's Faculty Study, Research and Travel Fund, skillfully administered by R. Francis Johnson, Dean of the Faculty. Much of the work was done during a sabbatical leave funded by Connecticut College. I hope that the appearance of this book justifies not only the college's support for scholarship but also the conviction that scholarship and teaching are inextricably interrelated.

I have presented preliminary versions of some of the material in invited lectures to members of the Honors Programs at La Salle University and Appalachian State University. I can now thank again John S. Grady and David P. Efroymson of La Salle and Thomas M. McLaughlin of Appalachian State for their kind invitations and for the the opportunity to present my ideas in such stimulating settings.

My wife has read very little of this book in manuscript. She has her own work to do. In her passionate commitment to her own goals and in the surpassing enthusiasm with which she works I have

found sustaining inspiration. It is only a very small
token of my feelings that I dedicate this book to her.

Mystic, Connecticut
23 June 1990

Understanding Religious Conversion

Whether encountered in the rendition of a country singer, a church choir, or in the haunting melody of a bagpiper; whether heard on the radio, in a concert, or at a religious service, "Amazing Grace" is one of the most widely known hymns in American culture. It may be heard or sung simply for pleasure or in the context of worship, but I will use it here to raise in vivid and succinct fashion the issue of religious conversion. The testimony in first verse of the hymn provides a dramatic example:

> Amazing grace! How sweet the sound
> That saved a wretch like me!
> I once was lost, but now am found,
> Was blind, but now I see.[2]

Several features of that account deserve comment. Of course, there is the graphic anonymous description of personal transformation. It implies a strong devaluation of the individual's previous status and an exaltation of the current status. Noteworthy also is the dependence on an outside agent. The transformation so briefly but forcefully recounted is not the result of any individual effort, of earnest reading or the diligent practice of self-help exercises; it was the result of grace—grace so sweet and sudden as to appear "amazing."

In this book I will examine experiences that appear to their subjects, and often to external observers as well, to be amazing. The experience of religious conversion is extraordinarily powerful in its effects on the lives of converts and on the lives of their families and friends. The conversion of many individuals can also have a profound impact on whole societies, even nations. The study of conversion can thus bring to light telling examples of how religion "works" in the lives of individuals and groups. Accordingly, this book has a double focus. Through examination of a series of individual cases, it describes and assesses the current status of the study of conversion. It also analyzes the contribution of the study of conversion to the general study of religion.

Though it depicts the singer's states before and after the transformation, "Amazing Grace" remains reticent about the details of the process itself. It seems, rather, designed to convince an audience that something mysterious, literally wonderful, occurred. Only in the fourth and final verse does the figure of "the Lord" appear; in the previous three verses grace itself acts upon the grateful singer. The academic study of religion, however, cannot remain satisfied with wonderment. It has to proceed beyond amazement to description, analysis, and interpretation.[3] Whether its specific subject is a personal transformation wrought by the grace of the Lord, an intense feeling of fellowship experienced during a ritual performance, a mystical insight into the heart of God, or any other human religious phenomenon, the academic study of religion seeks not to marvel, but to understand. Even if it describes something as amazing, it endeavors to explain precisely how and why that is so.

"Amazing Grace" both describes and interprets a process of personal transformation, a religious conversion. The change is portrayed in mutually exclusive, before-and-after, terms. A wretch who was once lost and blind is now found and can see. Overcoming "many dangers, toils, and snares," the individual in the hymn now has achieved relative safety and anticipates arriving home. Present safety and a safe conduct home are attributed to "the Lord," who will act as a "shield" for the individual "as long as life endures." The turning point in the dramatic transformation was "the hour I first believed."

Though there are many interesting things about "Amazing Grace,"—including its implicit theology, its past and current uses in religious worship and its continuing broad appeal beyond a specifically religious context—it serves here as a terse but inviting introduction to the topic of religious conversion. The hymn is both intriguing and puzzling—intriguing for its brief description of religious conversion, puzzling for its opacity and allusiveness. Beyond the sharp contrasts of the first verse and the image of the arduous journey, it is difficult to ascertain precisely which type of experience is being described in the hymn. The specific nature and workings of the grace that the hymn extols and their relations to the act of belief remain unclear, as do the character and activities of "the Lord" whose grace effects the transformation. Despite its seductive simplicity, in itself the hymn is anything but self-explanatory.

So it is with religious conversion. Whether the information comes from the testimonies so eagerly volunteered by converts themselves or reports elicited by workers in the field, whether the accounts are in the first or third person, whether the stories are carefully elaborated into spiritual autobiographies of impressive sophistication and length or must be pieced together out of artless replies to direct questions—in every case the facts of religious conversion present the observer with questions to be answered and problems to be solved. Converts may often simply want to evoke the observer's agreement that their transformation is indeed amazing, but sometimes they may even urge the observer to imitate their experience. Such, however, is not the way of the study of religion, which proceeds through the processes of description, analysis, and interpretation. It is true in this case, as it is generally, that whoever defines the questions defines the answers, and whoever identifies the problems identifies their acceptable solutions.

For the convert, one major question typically concerns others' willingness to duplicate the convert's experience. For example, in questioning recent converts to the independent African Apostolic Church of John Maranke, Bennetta Jules-Rosette always asked "Who gave you the news about this church?" One of her respondents quickly seized the opportunity to redefine the purpose of the interview and answered: "I gave it to you so you can adore God and your Savior Jesus."[4] Similarly, an early Christian *Discourse to the Greeks*, attributed to the second century teacher Justin, contains the exhortation, "Come, therefore, and be instructed. Become as I am, for I was once as you."[5] In a different vein, the recent memoirs of a former member of the Unification Church are presented as a cautionary tale about "the deceit, manipulation and terror which thousands of young Americans experience daily at the hands of modern cults."[6] That convert's tale is written in order to prevent conversion into the Unification Church and to promote "conversion" out of the group. Clearly, the goals that converts may have in recounting their experiences are not necessarily the goals that scholars or other students may have in investigating those experiences. In that sense alone it will be important to define carefully the questions that are being posed and to stipulate whose agenda is being followed.

The distinction between the convert's view from the inside and the academic observer's view from the outside is not the only one that needs to be made; nor is the distinction always that clear cut. The academic study of religious conversion has taken up a confusing welter of different questions and identified an overlapping tangle of different problems. Any treatment of conversion will depend, implicitly or explicitly, on various theoretical assumptions about religion, society, the individual, history, and other fundamental topics. Together, either in loose agglomeration or tight fit, those assumptions define a generic theory of religion, which guides all investigation. Such theories can be seen clearly in some work on religious conversion. William James' *The Varieties of Religious Experience* immediately comes to mind. In it, James explicitly develops a general theoretical perspective on religion and then considers the specific case of religious conversion from that general perspective. In other instances, perhaps the majority, the theoretical underpinnings of an investigation of religious conversion are more elusive. Arthur Darby Nock's classic treatment, *Conversion: the Old and the New in Religion from Alexander the Great to Augustine of Hippo,* is a case in point. Only with some difficulty can a general theory of religion be extricated from Nock's opening chapter, and even then it remains more a loose set of suggestions, which prepare the way for his careful treatment of the ancient evidence. In some cases, then, an explicit theoretical framework will define how conversion will be described, analyzed, and explained; in other cases, the specific acts of describing, analyzing, and explaining instances of conversion will imply a broader theoretical view of religion.

It is virtually impossible, then, to begin the study of religious conversion—or, for that matter, of anything—without a set of guiding questions. Those questions, in turn, are determined by the theoretical commitments and distinctive interests of the observer. Whether implicit or explicit, theories tell us what to look for, where to find it, and what to do with it. Theories enable us to choose, and choice is the only way to sort out from the multitude of possible examples the ones that may actually tell us something. To return to my initial example, theories and the questions they inspire offer a way to move beyond the simple assertion that the activity of "grace" is "amazing" and toward an understanding of precisely how and why, and for whom, that is the case. Theory makes possible description, analysis, and interpretation. Not to have some sort of overarching theoretical commitment is impossible; it is possible only to be more or less aware of what it is.

Since discussions of religious conversion are directed by prior theoretical commitments, they provide points of entry into questions that have animated the modern study of religion, such as the nature of religious experience, the personal or social nature of religion, and the contributions of religion to social stability and change. The study of conversion can thus become a laboratory for the study of religion. William James, for example, like Friedrich Schleiermacher before him, sets the question of religious experience squarely at center stage. James also forcefully argued that religion itself should be defined as "the feelings, acts, and experiences, of individual men in their solitude, so far as they apprehend themselves to stand in relation to whatever they may consider the divine."[7] That definition of religion as a radically individual pursuit casts James as the polar opposite of those who, like Emile Durkheim, would consider religion to be primarily social. Similarly, the emphasis on the transformative power of conversion, both for individuals and societies, raises again the question of the extent to which religion generally serves to promote and reinforce individual and social stability or to provoke individual and social transformation. Though such issues have sometimes been addressed in abstract theoretical terms, they have also been addressed in and through the study of specific data. Thus the study of religious conversion assumes broader signifi-cance insofar as it raises questions of fundamental importance for the study of religion.

In addition to its theoretical significance, several scholars have taken religious conversion to be the key to understanding more specific social and historical issues. For example, much of the popular and scholarly attention directed to "cults" or new religious movements in the United States, Canada, and Europe during the last few decades has focused on religious conversion. On the popular level that attention has produced a raft of lurid exposés, such as "I was a Robot for Sun Myung Moon" in the April, 1976 issue of *Glamour* magazine or "Darker Side of Sun Moon" in the June 14, 1976 issue of *Time*. On a somewhat more serious level are the cautionary tales of former members, such as Christopher Edwards' *Crazy for God* and Barbara and Betty Under-wood's *Hostage to Heaven*. There is also an extensive scholarly literature on the topic of conversion to new religious movements. Much of the literature, on all levels, shares the hope that the study of religious conversion can also produce insight into the particular character of American (or Canadian or European) society in the latter part of the twentieth century. As another example, in *Conversion* Arthur Darby Nock makes religious conversion the pivot around which a full understanding of the history of Christianity and Western Antiquity should turn. Similarly, Robin Horton has studied the importance of religious conversion for an understanding of the recent history of sub-Saharan Africa. Such examples show clearly how an understanding of religious conversion can be crucial to the investigation of broader social and historical developments.

Since there is no lack of data and no lack of interesting questions for the student of religious conversion, that student stands before a choice. Again, the decision to adopt a particular theoretical stance determines not only *what* material is chosen for description, analysis, and interpretation, but also *how* that material is understood.

I have chosen for this book a series of examples that demonstrate both the range of theoretical approaches to the study of conversion and the diversity of information about conversion itself. The theories will come from most of the disciplines that contribute to the study of religion, including psychology, philosophy, theology, sociology, anthropology, and history. The data will come from the ancient Mediterranean world, modern Africa, and the contemporary United States. Throughout this book, I will pursue several related goals. First, I will clarify the links between particular theoretical commitments and the interpretation of specific data. James' conception of religion as an affair of "individual men in their solitude," for example, decisively shapes his interpretation of conversion. I will pay specific attention to the reciprocal relationship between specific studies of religious conversion and the general theories about religion. Second, I will propose extended (re-)interpretations of several examples that have been prominent in the study of religious conversion. Each group of examples will be linked to a specific topic in the study of religious conversion, such as the nature of religious experience, the theological understanding of conversion, the formation of sociological models of the conversion process, and the role of conversion in broader cultural and historical change. The treatment of examples should be as important for *how* it proceeds as for *what* it achieves. Cases used to exemplify one approach might as easily be used to exemplify another. In fact, it would be an instructive exercise to test each of the examples against all of the theoretical approaches developed throughout the book. Third, I will clarify the contribution of the study of religious conversion to the study of religion in general, specific religious traditions, and specific social groups and historical periods. I want to demonstrate both the reach and the limits of such an analytical focus.

Religious conversion is not a prominent feature of many of the more widely-known definitions of religion. It is not necessarily implicit, for example, in Durkheim's characterization of a religion as "a unified system of beliefs and practices relative to sacred things, that is to say, things set apart and forbidden—beliefs and practices which unite into a single moral community . . . all those who adhere to them."[8] Nevertheless, Durkheim's focus on the social and symbolic character of religion will figure prominently in some interpretations of conversion. Similarly, the relation of religious conversion to Clifford Geertz's notion of a religion as a "system of symbols which acts to establish powrful, pervasive, and long-lasting moods and motivations in men by formulating conceptions of a general order of existence and clothing these conceptions with such an aura of factuality that the moods and motivations seem uniquely realistic"[9] is not immediately evident. Some of the scholars considered later in this book, however, will conceive of religions as systems of meaning and portray conversion as a change in world-view. Moreover, no explicit connection between Paul Tillich's definition of religion as "ultimate concern" and the phenomenon of conversion is readily apparent, but one Christian theologian, at least, has described conversion as "being grasped by ultimate concern."[10] Further, while James' definition of religion as "the feelings, acts, and experiences of individual men in their solitude" eventually proves to be quite in harmony with his interest in religious conversion, that interest is not directly required by his definition. But even if conversion has not been widely considered a fundamental defining characteristic of religion, as a category of religious action it impinges on a variety of topics of belief and practice. It offers an interesting starting point for the study of religion.

In the following chapters I will display and test some of the theories and methods adopted in the academic study of religion as they bear upon the description, analysis, and explanation of religious conversion. Although I have chosen a series of topics and examples from a relatively wide range of religious traditions, historical periods, and cultural and social situations, I make no effort to be all-inclusive in terms either of the material covered or of the theoretical questions raised.

Chapter one focuses on the topic of religious experience as it relates to conversion. For William James, as his definition of religion suggests, religious experience is the proper focus for the student of religion. Moreover, James argues that the study of religion should focus on "the original experiences which were the pattern-setters to all this mass of suggested feeling and imitated conduct. These experiences we can only find in individuals for whom religion exists not as a dull habit but as an acute fever rather."[11] It comes as no surprise, then, that James finds in the fervor of religious conversion those "hot" individuals who set the patterns for the duller masses. In this chapter I will first describe both James' theory of religion and his investigation of conversion. I will then consider James' views in light of the thorough critique offered by Wayne Proudfoot in his recent work, *Religious Experience*. Both theoretical views will be tested in a consideration of the religious experience of Malcolm X, as recounted in his autobiography. Malcolm's dramatic prison conversion—neither the first nor the last of that genre—will be the primary example of conversion in the first chapter.

Chapter two examines the theological understanding of religious conversion, particularly as it has been developed by Christian theologians. As my brief consideration of "Amazing Grace" suggests, conversion accounts can in some ways be considered theological assertions.[12] The hymn depends on a specific understanding of "grace," "the Lord," and belief for its full impact; moreover, it communicates the very theological concepts on which it depends. The theological understanding of conversion involves the elaboration within a specific tradition of the significance of the experience claimed. I will test a modern Christian theological understanding of conversion, that of Karl Barth in his *Church Dogmatics*, against Augustine of Hippo's account of his own conversion, which he tells in his *Confessions*—itself a sophisticated theological document.

Chapter three focuses on recent attempts to develop an adequate sociological model of the process of conversion, such as that developed in John Lofland and

Rodney Stark's influential article, "Becoming a World-Saver." Following Lofland and Stark, I will take as my primary data the conversion stories of current and former members of the Unification Church. Such "Moonies" and ex-"Moonies" have seldom been reluctant to tell the stories of their conversions. The Lofland-Stark model is an example of a theoretical understanding that is poles apart from James' concern for "individual men in their solitude."

Chapter four explores on what is, numerically at least, the most significant incidence of conversion in the modern world. Concomitant with the rise of colonialism in sub-Saharan Africa was the advance of Christianity. Purveyed by traders, colonial administrators, and missionaries, Christianity (along with Islam) has become one of the dominant religions in Africa. Since Christianity has been inextricably intertwined with the Western colonial endeavor from the outset, it has always been important to study any individual cases of conversion to Christianity within that broader colonial context. In the first part of the chapter I will consider the conversions of an American anthropologist and of native Africans to the independent Christian Apostolic Church of John Maranke. I will argue that those conversions raise questions both about presuppositions in various explanations of conversion and about the broader context of the phenomenon. The second part of this chapter will take up Robin Horton's provocative characterization of the development of Christianity and Islam in Sub-Saharan Africa as responses to the general trends of modernization.

Chapter five considers the role of conversion in historical change from another angle by focusing on the rise of Christianity in the ancient Mediterranean world. I will attempt to assess whether second century examples of conversion to Judaism (as portrayed in the romance *Joseph and Aseneth*), Christianity (Justin Martyr), philosophy (Lucian of Samosata), and the "mystery cult" of Isis (Apuleius) support Arthur Darby Nock's distinction between conversion as a decisive break with the past and a total psychological reorientation and adhesion as the mere adding of another to a stock of traditional beliefs. I will also consider the impact of Nock's general theory of religion on his characterization of conversion in the ancient world and assess Ramsay MacMullen's rather different recent attempt to explain the "Christianization" of the Roman Empire.

In the Conclusion I return to the broader question of

the study of conversion and the study of religion. I will show that just as the study of religious conversion is deeply influenced by prior theoretical considerations about the nature, function and value of religion, so also can the study of religion be influenced by attention to the study of religious conversion. I will also take up, as a negative example, the question of whether the category of conversion can be profitably used in the study of early Buddhism.

I do not intend to establish any *necessary* relationship between the theories and the examples considered in any given chapter. It is certainly possible, for example, to take Augustine's *Confessions* as evidence of the historical rise of Christianity in the ancient Mediterranean world, as Nock did, or to take Augustine as an example of individual religious experience, as James did. Similarly, it is possible to examine the theological understanding of conversion in the Unification Church either in the explanations of conversion offered by "Moonies" them-selves or in the more general reflections of Unification theologians.

References to background sources will be limited to what I consider to be the most helpful recent treatments in English. In general, the articles in the *Encyclopedia of Religion* will provide trustworthy guidance on topics such as "Malcolm X," "Manichaeism," "African Reli-gions" and the like. Beyond that, Lewis Rambo's article on "Conversion" in the same *Encyclopedia* and his full bibliography of "Current Research on Religious Conver-sion"[13] in provide sufficient initial suggestions for further reading.

William James, Chapter 1
Malcolm X, and Religious Experience

The interests of the general public and of the scholarly community in conversion have focused on often spectacular personal transformations. Especially when figures in the public eye, such as athletes or politicians, have announced their conversions, attention has centered on the experience itself, and frequently enough on its credibility. For example, sceptics of various stripes have wondered aloud whether Charles Colson, the former White House Special Counsel to Richard Nixon, or Eldridge Cleaver, the former revolutionary Black Panther leader, can really have been "born again."[14] Others have welcomed such stories as moving testimonies to divine power. In either case, individuals and the experiences they claim to have had become the primary topic for discussion.

Conversion necessarily raises in an acute form questions about the nature, function, and value of religious experience. As the first verse of "Amazing Grace" suggests, conversion is a category of action, whether conceived as something that *happens to* the convert or as something that the convert *does*. Whether it is viewed from a psychological, sociological, or theological perspective, conversion is frequently seen as involving a definite activity, a dramatic movement. In "Amazing Grace" it explicitly involves an act of salvation, a movement from being lost to being found, from being blind to attaining sight. Some sort of transformative experience, however described and understood, seems to lie at the center of the phenomenon of conversion.

William James' Theory of Conversion

Academic interpreters of conversion, despite wide differences in how they would understand it, have kept the issue of religious experience to the forefront. None has been more forceful or influential than William James. In *The Varieties of Religious Experience* James offers these characterizations of conversion:

> To be converted, to be regenerated, to receive grace, to experience religion, to gain an assurance, are so many phrases which denote the process, gradual or sudden, by which a self hitherto divided, and consciously wrong inferior and unhappy, becomes unified and consciously right superior and happy, in consequence of its firmer hold upon religious realities.[15]

> To say that a man is 'converted' means . . . that religious ideas, previously peripheral in his consciousness, now take a central place, and that religious aims form the habitual centre of his energy.[16]

What particularly interests James in conversion accounts are the "countless individual instances [of] an original and unborrowed experience."[17] That experience—of the unification of the self, of the movement of religious ideas from the periphery of consciousness to the center, of the energizing effect of those religious ideas—becomes for James what religion is all about. "What religion reports," James asserts, "always purports to be a fact of experience: the divine is actually present, religion says, and between it and ourselves relations of give and take are actual."[18] In one of his letters James simply characterizes experience as "all that sort of thing immediately and privately felt."[19] Conversion is a primary example of such immediate religious experience.

Indeed, James takes conversion and "melancholy" to be "the two main phenomena of religion."[20] To understand what he means by that striking assertion, it is necessary to take a closer look at James' general theory of religion. He claims that religion should be understood as "the feelings, acts, and experiences of individual men in their solitude, so far as they apprehend themselves to stand in relation to whatever they may consider the divine."[21] There are several noteworthy characteristics of that definition, but perhaps the most arresting, especially for those at all familiar with other definitions of religion, is its unwavering focus on the individual. As James puts it, he desires "to confine myself as far as I can to personal religion pure and simple."[22] The reasons for that decision are telling.

For James a fundamental division of the religious life is that between the personal and the institutional. Under the latter he would subsume all theology, ritual, and community organization; in short, anything he sees as involved in the "external art . . . of winning the favor of the gods"[23] is portrayed as a secondary elaboration of prior experience. As James puts the contrast: "Churches, when once established, live at second-hand upon tradition; but the *founders* of every church owed their power originally to the fact of their direct personal communion with the divine."[24] The original, direct, individual religious experience is what interests James. Everything else is second-hand, and consequently much less interesting.

But James is well aware that relatively few religious people can claim such "direct personal communion with the divine." Accordingly, he further limits his subject by dismissing as derivative the religious experience of the "ordinary believer." That too is "second-hand." The experience of such a person will be less revealing because "his religion has been made for him by others, communicated to him by tradition, determined to fixed forms by imitation, and retained by habit."[25] Little can be learned, James asserts, from such rote religion. His focus tightens further; theology, ritual, and community organization, and also the individual experience of the "ordinary believer" are swept aside. In their place

> we must make search rather for the *original experiences* which were the pattern-setters to all this mass of suggested feeling and imitated conduct. These experiences we can only find in individuals for whom religion exists not as a dull habit, but as an acute fever rather.[26]

With that, James' preliminary sketch of the object of his attention is completed. For him the study of religion should focus upon the "original experiences" of certain "fevered" personalities. Not only do their experiences create the pattern for the dull, ordinary believers, but they form the foundation on which the abstract edifices of theology, ceremony, and community are later erected.

James implicitly suggests that if the extraordinary experience of the religious genius is properly understood then everything else that is commonly associated with religion will be easily understood as well.[27] James' argument at this point depends on his clearly articulated assumption "that it always leads to a better understanding of a thing's significance to consider its exaggerations and perversions."[28] In the specific case of religious experiences he wants to concentrate on "that element or quality in them which we can meet nowhere else."[29] However they might be evaluated, James has made his principles of selection very clear. Given those principles, it is hardly surprising that *The Varieties* devotes extended consideration to conversion, saintliness, and mysticism. All can be treated as affairs of individual experience, and all are typical of the "fevered" experience on which James concentrates.

James' conception of what is interesting and important about religion leads him in a definite direction, not only to isolated individuals but specifically to their "feelings, acts, and experiences." The distinct character of each and the relations among them bear further consideration. In keeping with his turn away from theology, ritual, and community life, James asserts directly that "feeling is the deeper source of religion."[30] There is both a negative and a positive side to that assertion. The negative is already familiar; it enables James to dissociate the primary religious moment from its many secondary elaborations. The positive is more elusive. "Feeling" in itself scarcely seems specific enough; there would appear to be a vast array of common, and uncommon, human feelings. James' repeated rejection of the search for any single essence of religion[31] also makes is unlikely that he, in contrast to a theorist like Rudolf Otto in *The Idea of the Holy*,[32] would attempt to identify any specifically religious feeling as the core of religion. Rather, his positive understanding of feeling seems to depend upon its status as living, immediate, and authoritative. As James puts it:

> In the metaphysical and religious sphere, articulate reasons are cogent for us only when our inarticulate feelings of reality have already been impressed in favor of the same conclusion. . . . The unreasoned and immediate assurance is the deep thing within us, the reasoned argument is but a surface exhibition.[33]

James encapsulates his position in the proposition that "instinct leads, intelligence does but follow."[34]

At the root of religion, then, lies a direct, immediate apprehension of a dimension of reality. Since the initial feeling is inarticulate—and since, when it becomes articulate it is already being transformed into doctrine, ritual, myth, superstition or some other secondary facet of the religious life—it becomes very difficult to declare much more about that fundamental feeling other than its existence. Nonetheless, for James, "individuality is founded in feeling; and the recesses of feeling, the darker, blinder strata of character, are the only places in the world in which we catch real fact in the making."[35] Perhaps the closest that James comes to characterizing religious feeling is in his observation that a conviction of "the reality of the unseen" is fundamental to religion. The feelings, then, had by "individual men in their solitude" concern their direct, immediate, and authoritative encounter with the unseen realm. Consequently, James argues, "personal religious experience has its root and centre in mystical states of consciousness."[36] The particular experience, as James' cornucopia of case studies indicates, certainly varies from one individual to another, in accordance with the diversity of human character.[37]

For James, then, religion is foremost an individual experience. It flows from an immediate, inarticulate feeling, an intimation of the unseen order. An individual's religious experience is prior to any rational, intellectual understanding of it; it is experience, pure and simple. Experience may generate many of the familiar forms of the common religious life, but in itself it is prior to, and independent of, them. In that sense the "acts" that James includes in his definition of religion should be understood as being distinct from the common religious acts that make up second-hand religion. They refer more, for example, to the spontaneous prayer of the Christian convert seized by the Holy Spirit than to the regularized attendance at Sunday services.

James' sets forth an internally consistent, highly integrated, and quite distinctive approach to the study of religion. His basic propositions inform both the questions he asks and the answers that he proposes; they determine the type of material that he will look for and what he will do with it once he finds it. That influence of his theoretical commitment becomes even clearer when the second portion of his definition of religion is considered.

James is sufficiently wary of determining an essence of religion and sufficiently attentive to the diversity of human experience that he becomes quite circumspect in identifying the object of religion. The feelings, acts, and experiences of human beings are religious in so far as those individuals "apprehend themselves to stand in relation to whatever they may consider the divine."[38] Two aspects of that statement deserve comment. First, James is clearly unwilling to impose his own definition of "the divine" on the testimony of religious people. As was the case in identifying religious feelings or experiences, so it is in describing the divine. James makes the connection explicit:

> As there thus seems to be no one elementary religious emotion, but only a common storehouse of emotions upon which religious objects may draw, so there might conceivably also prove to be no one specific and essential kind of religious object, and no one specific and essential kind of religious act.[39]

In a rather direct fashion, James means to take people at their word. That leads to a second point. Not only does James hesitate to offer more than the most general characterization of the divine, he also insists on taking seriously the testimony of his informants as they present it. In an extended argument at the beginning of *The Varieties*, he rejects attempts to explain religion by reference to its origins. Echoing Jonathan Edwards, he asserts, "by their fruits ye shall know them, not by their roots."[40] James makes no Freudian excursion into the depths of the unconscious; for him, the operations of the human mind are open to direct scrutiny. That is especially true since James willingly confines himself "to those more developed subjective phenomena recorded in literature produced by articulate and fully self-conscious men."[41] Such comments provide further information about both the sources James will use and and the way that he will approach them. Personal accounts of religious experience will be of primary importance. Since James espouses a method that will see things *in* those words, not *through* them, the personal testimonies will need to be articulate and self-conscious to suit his purpose.

James' definition of religion includes a circumscription of the field of study, an identification of the crucial phenomena, a specification of type of evidence to be considered, and a description of the method to be followed. It thus allows him to formulate a program of investigation. He has told us what religion is, what it consists of, where it is to be found, and how it is to be studied. But he must move beyond his definition to tell us what it is all about.

The central issue that religion addresses is very simple. "Here is the real core of the religious problem: Help! help!"[42] In other words, James argues, religions universally seem both to recognize a sense of uneasiness and to propose a solution for it. Religions are efforts to identify and to solve perceived human problems. They assume that human beings need to and will call for help, that help exists, and that it can be delivered. To make matters more concrete, James proposes that "the pivot round which the religious life . . . revolves, is the interest of the individual in his private personal destiny."[43]

Though that interest might be expressed in concerns about a hereafter or some other post-mortem experience, James seems to have more in mind "the normal evolution of character [which] chiefly consist[s] in the straightening out and unifying of the inner self."[44] For James the unification of the divided self is the major contribution of religious belief, even though such unification may be accomplished in other ways, including the rejection of religion.[45] To understand the importance of the unification of the divided self, some appreciation of James' characterization of the two basic human temperaments is necessary. The "healthy-minded" temperament "has a constitutional incapacity for prolonged suffering, and . . . the tendency to see things optimistically."[46] A person so inclined resolutely focuses on the good in this world, refuses to make much of evil and sometimes even doubts that it exists at all. In contrast, the perspective of the "sick soul" tends to maximize the importance of evil and to locate it, not the good, at the core of human experience in the world. The healthy-minded, of course, need to be born only once in order to be happy; the sick souls need, however, to be born again. In psychological terms, "the twice-born character seems to [have] a certain discordancy or heterogeneity in the native temperament of the subject, an incompletely unified moral and intellectual constitution."[47] The sick soul is eminently in need of the crucial contribution of religion, since it "makes easy and felicitous what in any case is necessary,"[48] in this case some sort of reconciliation with a world teeming with acknowledged evil. James characterizes such a religious unification of self, or experience of rebirth in this way:

> He becomes conscious that this higher part [of the self] is conterminous and continuous with a MORE of the same quality, which is operative

in the universe outside of him, and which he can keep in working touch with, and in a fashion get on board of and save himself when all his lower being has gone to pieces in the wreck.[49]

The help sought thus comes from the "unseen reality;" its direct, immediate, and authoritative impact is felt and experienced by the religious individual, who subsequently gives testimony to that fact.

It should now be clearer both why James has studied conversion and why he has studied it as he has. Conversion represents a prime example of the unification of the divided self. The convert moves from a present sense of incompleteness and wrongness, from the agitation of the sick soul, to "the loss of all the worry, the sense that all is ultimately well with one, the peace, the harmony, the *willingness to be*, even though the outer conditions should remain the same."[50] The conversion experience "show[s] a human being what the high-water mark of his spiritual capacity is."[51] As such, it is a prime example of precisely the type of evidence James seeks, exaggerated, "hot" religious experiences, which display the distinctive characteristics of religion most clearly. With that in mind, it is now possible to assess James' understanding of conversion in light of his general theory of religion.

In the midst of his discussion of conversion James notes "the admirable congruity of Protestant theology with the structure of the mind as shown in such experiences."[52] As I will show, there may well be several ways to interpret that statement, but for James it reveals the superior ability of Protestant theology to speak to the crisis of the sick soul. Of course, since James depicts religious experience as direct, immediate, authoritative, and unconditioned by prior beliefs, he is led to describe the similarities he perceives as an "admirable congruity." Yet they can be read in another, admittedly more suspicious, fashion.

A Critique of James

In *Religious Experience* Wayne Proudfoot disputes the proposition that religious experience is independent of, and prior to, specific beliefs and practices. Proudfoot

argues throughout his book that "there is no uninterpreted experience."[53] He claims that

> our experience is already informed and consti-
> tuted by our conceptions and tacit theories
> about ourselves and our world. All observation
> is theory-laden. We can design procedures in
> which certain hypotheses can be tested, but any
> perception or experience is already shaped by
> the concepts and implicit judgments we bring
> to it. [54]

Proudfoot conveniently tests his position against the first
report of conversion that James considers in *The
Varieties*.

James begins with "the quaint case of an unlettered
man, Stephen H. Bradley, whose experience is related in
a scarce American pamphlet."[55] In that tract Bradley
recounts his initial vision of Jesus Christ as Savior,
which occurred when he was fourteen years old. For
some time Bradley took that vision to be his conversion
experience. In language reminiscent of "Amazing
Grace," Bradley describes his selfishness and self-right-
eousness prior to that moment and his subsequent
burning desire to forgive his enemies and contribute to
the welfare of humankind. He seeks as well to become
the vehicle of salvation for others. Some nine years
later, however, Bradley is challenged to testify to the
certainty of his convictions by participants in a local
religious revival. In response to their queries, he replies
that he hopes that he had religion, but their questions
seem to provoke a nagging doubt. Soon thereafter he
attends the service of a Methodist preacher, whose vivid
description of the coming judgment impresses, but does
not move, the twenty-three year old Bradley. On
returning home, Bradley has an experience which he
attributes to the activity of the Holy Spirit. His heart
begins to beat very quickly; he feels a sense of elation,
coupled with a definite impression of humility and
unworthiness. He feels "a stream (resembling air in
feeling)" come into his mouth, though he had not
ingested anything. As the experience continues, he
begins to consider what it might mean. At that point
young Bradley sees in a vision the New Testament,
opened to Romans 8:26-27. He reads the lines that
promise the Spirit's aid for human infirmities, groans,
and is interupted by his brother, who had been aroused
from sleep in the bedroom next door. Bradley's heart
rate slows as he reflects on his experience. He feels
himself to be full of the Holy Spirit, and after a brief

prayer of thanksgiving falls finally to sleep. He wakes the next morning with a feeling of religious exaltation and searches for a New Testament, in order to confirm his vision. Bradley tells his parents of his experience, comparing himself to the apostles at Pentecost. After breakfast, he makes the rounds of his neighbors to converse with them about religion.

Though James, by the brevity of his comments, indicates that the meaning of Bradley's conversion story is self-evident, it is not clear how he wants Bradley's testimony to be understood. James simply introduces Bradley's case as a "concrete example" of the process of conversion, noting that "it shows how in these inner alterations one may find one unsuspected depth below another."[56] The Bradley testimony does furnish vivid instances of what James takes to be the hallmarks of religious conversion: a direct personal encounter with the perceived divine, the attendant physical perturbations, and the ensuing conviction of certainty, solidity, and direction. As Proudfoot indicates, Bradley's testimony can show many other things as well, many of them distinctly at odds with James' sketchy interpretation.

As with James, Proudfoot's eye is drawn to Bradley's physical distress. But where James tacitly acccepted Bradley's description and explanation of his conversion experience, implying that there was a self-evident connection between Bradley's bodily symptoms and the Christian Holy Spirit, Proudfoot sees the possibility of distinguishing Bradley's physical experience and his attribution of its cause to the Holy Spirit. By noting that Bradley's conversion testimony contains an explanation of his experience, Proudfoot is able to clarify the sources and context of that explanation. He observes that

> Bradley, like so many prospective devotees before and since, could not understand his feelings in naturalistic terms. Religious symbols offered him an explanation that was compatible both with his experience and with his antecedent beliefs. He did not consider explanations involving Krishna, Zeus, or the Qur'an. The content of the scripture and the experience of being moved or physiologically aroused were confidently linked.[57]

In his interpretation Proudfoot emphasizes the events that preceded Bradley's transforming experience. Prior beliefs (e.g., in the Christian Holy Spirit), practices (attending the revivalist's meeting), and experiences (his "conversion" at age fourteen), Proudfoot argues, conditioned Bradley's interpretation of his racing heart and other physical symptoms. Had Bradley only recently returned from a meeting of people with heart ailments, his interpretation of his own experience might well have been different. Accordingly, Proudfoot proposes that "any bodily changes or feelings may be accounted for in religious terms when the subject's past experience and present context makes such an account plausible and compelling."[58] Contrary to James, Proudfoot argues that "emotions assume particular concepts and beliefs. They cannot be assimilated to sensations or simple internal events that are independent of thought."[59]

Proudfoot's analysis of Bradley's conversion story shows that there is no necessary connection between Bradley's testimony and James' specific interpretation. Simply put, James *has chosen* to interpret Bradley's testimony in a certain way. Guided by his own theory of religion, James sees in Bradley's account the religious experience of an individual in isolation. Yet Bradley himself provides information about his prior history, the immediate social and religious circumstances of his conversion, and the new social relationships that he begins to form in its wake. James simply emphasizes certain aspects of the account at the expense of others. So does Proudfoot. James' theoretical assumptions, which may also have been influenced by his personal acquaintance with the individualistic Protestant tradition,[60] lead him to decide that certain elements of Bradley's account are more important than others. Similarly, Proudfoot's different theoretical commitments lead him to emphasize the value of other portions of the testimony as evidence. Their divergent interpretations clearly show that there is no necessary connection between any one interpretation and Bradley's account itself. One can determine what it is "really about" only within the context of a set of theoretical assumptions. Those assumptions determine what kinds of questions will be asked. James inquires about Bradley's personal experience. Proudfoot wants to know how and why Bradley came to describe and interpret his experience as he did. Their questions, in turn, direct each observer to certain elements of the testimony, rather than others. Thus the questions themselves implicitly indicate the type of evidence and even the answers that will be acceptable. Bradley's testimony "means something" to

Bradley, to James, and to Proudfoot. But the context in which meaning is sought differs in each instance.

In Proudfoot's view, Bradley's attribution of his physical symptoms to the Christian Holy Spirit is not something that comes *after* the experience itself. The experience and the judgment about its cause cannot be so easily separated. The experience and the attribution of its cause are bound up together, since "we constantly monitor our actions as well as our feelings and make causal attributions that enter into the determination of our experience and that have direct behavioral consequences. Beliefs about the causes of one's experience are themselves constitutive of the experience."[61] Bradley himself notes at several points in his narrative that he was actively seeking a plausible explanation of what was happening to him; he simply does not present the details of his immediate context and prior experience as crucial elements in his explanation of his conversion; he skips over them to arrive at his theological explanation. Similarly, James skips over the same details in developing his psychological explanation of Bradley's conversion. For Proudfoot, however, those same details of prior history and current circumstances provide the key to explaining Bradley's account. Because Bradley was who he was, Proudfoot argues, a person with a distinctive history in a specific situation and who held certain beliefs, his interpretation of his physical symptoms as the activity of the Christian Holy Spirit could virtually be predicted.

In a direct reversal of James' argument, Proudfoot asserts that beliefs are indeed prior to and constitutive of experience. In the particular case of mysticism, along with conversion and saintliness one of James' three main forms of religious life, Proudfoot contends that

> the experience is shaped by a complex pattern
> of concepts, commitments, and expectations
> which the mystic brings to it. These beliefs and
> attitudes are formative of, rather than conse-
> quent upon, the experience. They define in
> advance what experiences are possible.[62]

Given his own concepts, commitments, and expectations, it hardly seems possible that Bradley would attribute his racing heart to the activity of Krishna, Zeus, or the Qur'an. Nor was he very likely to attribute his physical experience to some non-religious factors in his social, psychological, or sexual life. Bradley was prepared by his past life and present circumstances to understand his experience in a certain way; indeed, he could scarcely do otherwise.

Though Proudfoot privileges certain parts of Bradley's testimony as providing the interpretive key, he does not ignore the testimony about the moment of conversion. Rather, he tries to bring together Bradley's past and present into a coherent and consistent explanation. To the extent that he is successful, Proudfoot surpasses James by offering a fuller and therefore more satisfying interpretation of the narrative that Bradley has written. James' interpretation suffers not only because of its brevity but also because of its constricted focus. James' theory of religion implies a judgment of what is important in accounts like Bradley's and leads him simply to ignore certain elements of the text. If, by definition, religious experience is immediate, autonomous, authoritative, and prior to any elaboration in doctrine, ritual, or community life, Bradley's earlier "conversion" at age fourteen, his participation in the revival, and even his prior Christian faith are not strictly relevant to the explanation of his conversion. Above all, what is important for James about Bradley's conversion is the inner experience it indicates. By deciding *what* is to be explained, James decides *how* it is to be explained. The same holds true for Proudfoot, of course, but in this specific instance his explanation is more satisfying because it demonstrates a much more comprehensive grasp of the details of the example at hand. Where Bradley's own explanation of his conversion resolves into a theological assertion and James' explanation severs Bradley from both his past and his continuing life in the world, Proudfoot's explanation takes better account of past and present, experience and interpretation, society, personality, and theology.

Proudfoot extends his argument to include the proposal that the distinguishing mark of religious experience is precisely that it includes "an embedded claim" about its own cause. That is, the experience in question is defined as a *religious* experience and consequently not a physical, sexual, psychological, social, or any other type of experience. In Bradley's case that claim is evident in the assertion that his conversion was the result of the activity of the Holy Spirit. Proudfoot's critique of the tradition in religious thought and the study of religion that holds religious experience to be immediate, autonomous, and independent of belief and practice poses a serious challenge not only to James' view of conversion but also to the general theory of religion on which it is founded. It suggests that even a narrow focus on "individual men in their solitude" needs to be tempered by a recognition of the formative role that language and beliefs, and through them society, culture, and history, have upon individual "feelings, acts, and experiences." It specifically calls into question James' contention that "religious experience . . . spontaneously and inevitably engenders myths, supersitions, dogmas, creeds, and metaphysical theologies."[63] In fact, the relationship may be the opposite.

In light of Proudfoot's critique, James' observation about the "admirable congruity" between Protestant theology and the "structure of the mind" revealed in many of the conversion testimonies in *The Varieties* can be seen in a rather different light. It is precisely because Protestant theology (with its attendant beliefs, practices, and forms of life, etc.) *has already* structured the minds, and hence the experiences, of the converts that their testimonies take the forms they do. What is "admirable" or impressive in those stories, at least in terms of Proudfoot's analysis, is not so much a serendipitous correlation between theology and experience but rather the repeated dramatization of the immense power of religious belief to shape, channel, and even create experience. Proudfoot thus offers a compelling alternative to James' understanding of religion.

Appropriate respect for James' passion for the concrete, however, suggests that the matter not be left solely on the level of theory. It was the evidence that he considered, James reports, that led him to frame his discussion of conversion the way that he did. To test his theories, and the alternative suggested by Proudfoot, it is necessary to consider concrete data. To avoid the possibility that the Protestant theology that suffuses his sources may have skewed James' investigations, a conversion testimony from a somewhat different realm will be considered.

Malcolm X's Conversion

Few leaders in the African-American community have ever provoked as much shock, fear, and hatred among white Americans as Malcolm X. A well-schooled hustler from the mean streets of Roxbury and Harlem, who received the distinctive anti-white teachings of Elijah Muhammed's Nation of Islam while imprisoned for burglary, Malcolm X became the most prominent spokesman and missionary for that movement of African-American pride, hope, and reaction until his acrimonious split with Elijah Muhammed. When he was assassinated on February 18, 1965, he was struggling in the face of opposition both from his former co-religionists and from white society to establish the Organization for Afro-American Unity, a new "non-religious and non-sectarian" group whose tenets not only represented a move away from Malcolm X's former condemnation of the white man as the devil but also the transformative effect of his recent pilgrimage to Mecca and subsequent travels in Africa.

Malcolm Little's prison conversion to the Nation of Islam and his subsequent espousal of a more orthodox Islam certainly fit James' description of conversion as a process in which "religious ideas, previously peripheral in his consciousness, now take a central place, and . . . religious aims form the habitual centre of his energy."[64] The young Malcolm had had ample exposure to various kinds of religion, first through his father's preaching,[65] then through his mother's association with Seventh Day Adventists,[66] and also through visits to the services of "Holy Rollers" with the family with whom he was placed by the state after his mother's institutionalization.[67] None of that early exposure to forms of Protestant Christianity in the United States, however, evoked in the young Malcolm any explicit religious response; religion remained peripheral, at best, to the center of his energy. What impressed Malcolm Little most in his youth, and continued to do so throughout his life, were the signs of racism, from cutting remarks to burning crosses, which reminded him daily that in the eyes of most white people he was inferior.

The *Autobiography* describes as "the first major turning point" of his life an incident that indelibly impressed that conviction on a young seventh-grader. It concerns a conversation between Malcolm Little and an English teacher who, before that, had seemed very concerned and helpful:

> He told me, "Malcolm, you ought to be thinking about a career. Have you been giving it thought?"
>
> The truth is, I hadn't. I never have figured out why I told him, "Well, yes, sir, I've been thinking I'd like to be a lawyer." Lansing had no Negro lawyers—or doctors either—in those days, to hold up an image I might have aspired

to. All I really knew for certain was that a
lawyer didn't wash dishes, as I was doing.

Mr. Ostrowski looked surprised, I remember,
and leaned back in his chair and clasped his
hands behind his head. He kind of half-smiled
and said, "Malcolm, one of life's first needs is
for us to be realistic. Don't misunderstand me,
now. We all here like you, you know that. But
you've got to be realistic about being a nigger.
A lawyer—that's no realistic goal for a nigger.
You need to think about something you *can* be.
You're good with your hands—making things.
Everybody admires your carpentry shop work.
Why don't you plan on carpentry? People like
you as a person—you'd get all kinds of work."

The more I thought afterwards about what
he said, the more uneasy it made me. It just
kept treading around in my mind.

What made it really begin to disturb me was
Mr. Ostrowski's advice to others in my class—
all of them white. . . . They all reported that
Mr. Ostrowski had encouraged what they
wanted. Yet nearly none of them had earned
marks equal to mine.

It was a surprising thing that I had never
thought of it that way before, but I realized
that whatever I wasn't, I *was* smarter than
nearly all of those white kids. But apparently I
was still not intelligent enough, in their eyes, to
become whatever *I* wanted to be.

It was then that I began to change—inside.[68]

The realization that even his professed friends and
supporters in white society could countenance for him
only a limited choice of professions, and hence public
identities, becomes and remains a fundamental perception for Malcolm. His situation can easily be described
in James' terms. Racism causes the "sickness" in
Malcolm's soul; it provokes the uneasiness for which he
seeks a solution. When he seeks help, either in the form
of an understanding of his situation or an antidote to it,
the help must address the continuing problem of racism.
James might also point to the early "subconscious
incubation" of questions and motivations that will play
significant roles in Malcolm's later conversion to the
Nation of Islam.[69] Yet it is important to note that while
Malcolm will focus on incidents from his own life as
they concern what James would call his "private
personal destiny," he consistently understands them as

examples of a much broader social and historical pattern. It is just such broader contexts that James' theory of religion leads him to ignore. More so than in the case of Stephen Bradley, James' narrow focus would lead him to miss what Malcolm sees as the crucial dimensions of his conversion.

Take, for example, Malcolm's brief anecdote about stealing apples:

> Sometimes, instead of going home from school, I walked the two miles up the road into Lansing. I began drifting from store to store, hanging around outside where things like apples were displayed in boxes and barrels and baskets, and I would watch my chance and steal me a treat. You know what a treat was to me? Anything![70]

In contrast to the story about the theft of pears in Augustine of Hippo's *Confessions*, which will be examined in the next chapter, Malcolm's act does not prod him into a flurry of introspection. Malcolm knows why he took the apples; he was hungry. The incident does not lead Malcolm to any prolonged consideration of sin, self, and soul. Rather, it takes its place in a litany of hunger, as one more indication of the "psychological deterioration"[71] that set upon the Little family after the death of Malcolm's father. Significantly, Malcolm locates the source of the problem (theft, in this case) outside of himself and outside of his family. White racists had murdered his father; a (white) insurance company had failed to pay the substantial death benefits on a large policy, claiming that Earl Little had killed himself; as the savings ran out, older children went out to work and Malcolm's mother turned to credit and then to welfare. Economic, physical, and psychological deteriorations reinforced each other. The separation of the siblings into various foster homes and the institutionalization of Malcolm's mother completed the destruction of the Little family. In Malcolm's words:

> I truly believe that if ever a state social agency destroyed a family, it destroyed ours. We wanted and tried to stay together. Our home didn't have to be destroyed. But the Welfare, the courts, and their doctor, gave us the one-two-three punch. And ours was not the only case of this kind.[72]

In his narrative of his early years Malcolm attends at least as much to the division, demoralization, and destruction of his family as he does to himself. He does not and cannot sever himself from the social groups of which he is part.

Malcolm cannot separate his life, and the process of conversion within it, from its social context precisely because he sees and experiences the overwhelming influence of that context on his life. He does not locate the problem for which he seeks "help" within himself, as did so many of James' subjects, but outside himself, in society and history. His *Autobiography*, therefore, does not fit the pattern of conversion that James describes in *The Varieties*. In fact, James' understanding of conversion proves to be even less adequate for the interpretation of Malcolm's testimony than it was for Bradley's conversion story. Malcolm is remarkably reticent about his personal religious experience, at least as James defines the term. He is quite voluble, however, about his new religious convictions and about the new view of the world that he adopts with his conversion to the Nation of Islam.

As Proudfoot's reinterpretation of Bradley's conversion story shows, James' understanding of conversion encounters problems on both the theoretical and practical levels. Proudfoot has skillfully exposed the theoretical difficulties with James' approach. The practical problems become all the more evident when one attempts to apply James' theoretical understanding of conversion to Malcolm X's *Autobiography*. Like Stephen Bradley's, Malcolm's description and interpretation of his conversion are shaped by his prior understanding of his own situation. But the dimensions of that situation for Malcolm are primarily social and historical, not personal; he focuses upon the plight of all black people in a white society. Malcolm X *sees and consequently experiences* the world in quite a different way. Malcolm's insistence on the social and historical dimensions of his experience frustrates any attempt to treat Malcolm as an individual in isolation. Even if such an approach were theoretically possible and advisable, it would founder on the evidence at hand. To wrest Malcolm from those contexts, as James' approach demands, is to miss the point, as Malcolm sees it, of his public and private lives.

Since Malcolm's beliefs and experiences are different from Bradley's, so also is his understanding of his own conversion. As Proudfoot succinctly puts it, "those in different traditions have different experiences."[73] If that is the case, James' understanding of conversion, which is developed largely on the basis of examples from a single tradition, will not necessarily be adequate for the description, analysis, and interpretation of examples from another tradition.

The testimonies on which James focuses in *The Varieties* repeatedly portray conversion as the act of an individual in isolation. They provide extensive support for James' specific theory of conversion and his general theory of religion. Without doubt, they display a remarkable congruity with Protestant theological convictions. But those convictions, and the way that they shape conversion accounts, are specific to the Protestant (and Christian) tradition. To the extent that James' *theoretical* understanding of conversion depends upon the dominant *theological* and therefore experiential understanding of conversion within the Protestant tradition, it will be inadequate to the description, analysis, and interpretation of conversion accounts from other traditions. The narrow range of data that James considers leads him to formulate generalizations that are inadequate to the task of formulating a general theory of conversion and of religion. A more thorough investigation of Malcolm's testimony will bear that out.

Malcolm's initial summary of his conversion is brief and direct: "I found Allah and the religion of Islam and it completely transformed my life."[74] That simple statement, of course, conceals a complicated process, a process that brings back to the fore many of the themes from Malcolm's early life: his close ties to his family, the impact of racism on Malcolm, the Little family, and all black people, Malcolm's native intelligence and desire to put it to good use, even the importance of dietary prohibitions, initially urged on Malcolm by his mother for different, non-Islamic, reasons.

Malcolm first met the Nation of Islam in a letter from his brother Philbert. In a previous letter Philbert had informed his brother that his "holiness" church back in Detroit was praying for him and Malcolm had responded with a tirade against religion. In a second letter soon after, Philbert apparently described his conversion to the "natural religion for the black man," the Nation of Islam. Malcolm remained hostile. Only when a letter from his brother Reginald arrived was Malcolm's interest aroused; the reason is clear: "Malcolm, don't eat any more pork, and don't smoke any more cigarettes." Reginald wrote, "I'll show you how to get out of prison."[75] Three or four days later, the beginnings of Malcolm's conversion manifested themselves in concrete action:

> I wasn't even thinking about pork when I took my seat at the long table. Sit-grab-gobble-stand-file out; that was the Emily Post in prison eating. When the meat platter was passed to me, I didn't even know what the meat was; usually, you couldn't tell, anyway— but it was suddenly as though *don't eat any more pork* was flashed on a screen before me.
>
> I hesitated, with the platter in mid-air; then I passed it along to the inmate waiting next to me. He began serving himself; abruptly he stopped. I remember him turning, looking surprised at me.
>
> I said to him, "I don't eat pork." . . .
>
> It made me proud in some odd way. One of the universal images of the Negro, in prison and out, was that he couldn't do without pork. It made me feel good to see that my not eating it had especially startled the white convicts.[76]

It is clear from a variety of comments Malcolm makes that he was most intrigued by the connection between abstaining from pork and getting out of prison. It is only later that he understands that incident as his "first pre-Islamic submission" to the will of God.[77] In retrospect, the experience becomes religious. As Proudfoot remarks about the convert: "once involved in action, he is more susceptible to adopting the beliefs of the community in order to justify his actions and explain his feelings."[78] Only gradually does Malcolm arrive at a more sophisticated, and more Islamic, understanding of the links that Reginald saw between not eating pork and getting out of prison. In the process Malcolm will abandon an alternative explanation, his initial hunch that abstaining from pork and cigarettes might provoke psychological or physical symptoms that would force his release from prison.

Malcolm's conversion, then, includes both a commitment to certain types of action and the acceptance of a system of beliefs. The two processes occur simultaneously, and it is difficult to weight the importance of one more heavily than the other. The practices Malcolm adopts give him a distinctive identity, both in the eyes of his fellow convicts and in the eyes of his family. The beliefs that he adopts set his current situation and that of black people in general within an all-encompassing historical and mythological framework. Belief and practice, the personal, social, and historical, blend together to offer Malcolm a new identity and a new understanding of his place in the world. In many ways, Malcolm's conversion is an act of the will; he decides to act in certain ways and he decides to accept certain beliefs. James includes such conversions in his *volitional* type and distinguishes them from conversions that involve *self-surrender*.[79] I would contend, however, that those are more types of *explanation* than types of *experience*, if experience is understood with James to be whatever is immediately and privately felt. In my view, James is describing and classifying converts' interpretations of their own experiences, at least as much as the immediate experiences themselves. In accordance with his theoretical presuppositions, James virtually ignores the interpretative component of reports of religious experience. Proudfoot, however, has shown clearly that reports of religious experience, not the least by describing the experience in question *as religious*, contain elements of an interpretation of that experience. Subjects use their own tacit theoretical frameworks to understand and give meaning to what they experience. In Proudfoot's words, "any experience assumes particular concepts, beliefs, hypotheses, and theories about ourselves and the world"[80] that are shaped by the subject's past experience and present context. To shift the focus of inquiry from experience to explanation makes it easier to set instances of religious conversion into their historical and cultural contexts and it also clarifies the relationship between explanations offered by outside obervers and those preferred by converts themselves.

The themes that reveal the historical and cultural contexts of Malcolm X's conversion and that Malcolm himself will make part of his explanation of his conversion to the Nation of Islam are clearly articulated in one of Reginald's conversations with his brother:

> You don't even know who you are . . . . You don't even know, the white devil has hidden it from you, that you are of a race of people of ancient civilizations, and riches in gold and kings. You don't even know your true family name, you wouldn't recognize your true language if you heard it. You have been cut off by the devil white man from all true knowledge of your own kind. You have been a victim of the evil of the devil white man ever since he murdered and raped and stole you from your

native land in the seeds of your
forefathers. . . .[81]

Malcolm's concern about an identity being foisted on
him by others goes back at least to his encounter with
his seventh-grade English teacher, "the first major
turning point" of his life. In the messenger of Allah,
Reginald claims, Malcolm will see "a black man, like
us."[82] Later on, Malcolm X himself will preach that
"the Honorable Elijah Muhammad is giving us a true
identity, and a true position—the first time they have
ever been *known* to the American black man!"[83] The
demonization of the white man becomes part of a full,
mythological explanation for both the personal experience and the historical pattern of racism with which
Malcolm is so familiar. The phrase about "riches in
gold and kings" evokes the possibility of an alternative, a
paradise obscured in the past that might be reached
again. The mention of a "true family name" connects
with Malcolm's early observations about his mother's
light skin and mixed background;[84] with the notion of a
"true language," it evokes the image of a home and a
homeland where things were in their proper order, an
antidote for the feelings of dislocation and domination.
Certainly, the mention of murder directs Malcolm back
to the murder of his own father and the consequent
destruction of his family, while the mention of rape
again recalls his mother's origin in the willful actions of
her white, slave-holding father. Thus the summary that
Reginald provides of the teachings of the Nation of
Islam speaks directly and distinctly to Malcolm's prior
experience and current situation, as well as to the
experience and situation of every black person. As
Malcolm puts it: "The teachings ring true—to every
Negro"[85] and " 'The white man is the devil' is a perfect
echo of that black convict's lifelong experience."[86] The
Nation of Islam offers Malcolm an overarching historical
and mythological explanation of the state of the world, a
compelling explanatory context for his own life, and a
hope for change. It prescribes as well specific behavior
that will disengage Malcolm from society, make him a
member of a separate community, and make possible the
realization of his immediate and ultimate goals.

Islam, "the true knowledge of the black man," offers
Malcolm a new life. He remembers being amazed both
at how quickly he was able to move toward that new life
and at how difficult it was to accept it. On the one
hand, "Every instinct of the ghetto jungle streets, every
hustling fox and criminal wolf instinct in me, which

would have scoffed at and rejected any thing else, was struck numb. It was as though all of that life merely was back there, without any remaining effect, or influence."[87] On the other, "I was going through the hardest thing, also the greatest thing, for any human being to do; to accept that which is already within you, and around you."[88] As the *Autobiography* presents it, then, Malcolm Little's transformation into Malcolm X unfolds slowly, from his first, nearly unconscious gesture of abstaining from pork, through his extensive conversations with his brother and his own agonizing consideration of the strange, new message,[89] to his dawning acceptance, through his subsequent tutelage by Elijah Muhammad by correspondance and his own voracious reading. Malcolm finds in the teachings of the Nation of Islam "true knowledge,"[90] and the truth makes him free: "I had never been so truly free in my life."[91]

Malcolm Little's entrance into the Nation of Islam, however, was not the end of his religious transformation. Both the community he entered and the teachings he accepted would within a few years be called into question. Malcolm rose quickly in the hierarchy of the Nation of Islam, becoming Elijah Muhammad's primary lieutenant and receiving teaching directly from him.[92] He professed a fierce loyalty to the leader of the Nation of Islam, but he gave up that loyalty and became a pariah among Elijah Muhammad's followers when he could not remain silent about the leader's moral failings and hypocrisy. Malcolm's discovery of Elijah Muhammad's adultery began his departure from the Nation of Islam. The response of the community, and particularly the hierarchy, to Malcolm's discovery sealed the split. At that crucial juncture, Malcolm discovered a positive alternative to the Nation of Islam.

During the turmoil prompted by his departure from the Nation of Islam, Malcolm resolved to bring to fruition a long-cherished dream, to make the pilgrimage to Mecca (the "Hajj"). In the process he would come face to face with what many Arab, Middle Eastern, and North African Muslims who had heard him speak described as "true Islam." That dramatic confrontation, in the context of his pilgrimage, would cause Malcolm to reformulate his ideology, a task still in process at the time of his assassination. Malcolm's pilgrimage to Mecca constitutes, in effect, his second conversion. His encounter with Muslims from all nations and walks of life had a profound impact on him. During the pilgrimage "All ate as One, and slept as One. Everything about the pilgrimage atmosphere accented the Oneness of Man under One God."[93] As a result, Malcolm was driven to reconsider one of the primary tenets of the Nation of Islam, that the white man is the devil. During the Hajj, Malcolm relates,

> . . . I first began to perceive that "white man," as commonly used, means complexion only secondarily; primarily it described attitudes and actions. In America, "white man" meant specific attitudes and actions toward the black man, and toward all other non-white men. But in the Muslim world, I had seen that men with white complexions were more genuinely brotherly than anyone else had ever been.[94]

Malcolm's "second conversion," which brings him into the *umma* (community) of orthodox Islam, makes him a part of an international community with which he will have progressively stronger relations and also tempers his anti-white rhetoric, replacing it with a vision of the potential for peaceful relations among people of all races. His indictment of racism will henceforth focus more directly on the specific practices and policies of American society than on a stark black-white racial contrast.

Again, in his "second conversion" certain experiences of Malcolm's have a definite force. The people massed for the flight from Frankfurt to Cairo make a deep impression:

> Throngs of people, obviously Muslims from everywhere, bound on the pilgrimage, were hugging and embracing. They were of all complexions, the whole atmosphere was of warmth and friendliness. The feeling hit me that there really wasn't any color problem here. The effect was as though I had just stepped out of a prison.[95]

The excitement intensifies as the pilgrims prepare to leave Cairo for Jedda, the gateway to Mecca:

> . . . we all had begun intermittently calling out "*Labbayka! Labbayka!*" (Here I come, O Lord!) The airport sounded with the din of *Muhrim* expressing their intention to perform the journey of the Hajj.[96]

Again, Malcolm experiences a sense of unity that overcomes racial distinctions: "Packed in the plane were white, black, brown, red, and yellow people, blue eyes and blond hair, and my kinky red hair—all together, brothers! All honoring the same God Allah, all in turn giving equal honor to each other."[97] Just as his initial encounter with the Nation of Islam, the experience of the pilgrimage "has forced me to *re-arrange* much of my thought-patterns previously held, and to *toss aside* some of my previous conclusions."[98] It might be instructive to describe this transition as Malcolm's conversion from "Black Muslim" to "black Muslim."

At many points the religious career of Malcolm X seems to be susceptible to description and analysis in terms of James' general theory of religion and specific understanding of the process of conversion. His prison conversion accomplishes for Malcolm a unification of a divided self; it gives him a way to use his mind, a personal and social identity, a community and prescribed form of behavior. His pilgrimage to Mecca certainly remains the "high-water mark" of his spiritual experience. Yet, just as in the case of Stephen Bradley, it is difficult to proceed with James in identifying Malcolm's religious experience as direct, immediate, and unconditioned by his beliefs and practices. As he recounts it in the *Autobiography*, Malcolm's prison conversion was preceded by a long string of revealing incidents which convinced him that the fundamental problem in his life, and in the lives of all black people, was the historical pattern of white racism. That knowledge defined Malcolm's sense of "uneasiness;" it identified the problem for which he sought "help." It constituted the pivot around which his "personal private destiny" revolved, but neither the problem nor the destiny was peculiar to Malcolm. The form of Malcolm's initial conversion, then, like Bradley's, was shaped well beforehand. His previous ideas and commitments determine the shape that his conversion will take. It is hard indeed to imagine Malcolm assenting to a doctrine or joining a group that holds that the historical domination of the black people by the white is of little moment. Malcolm's *religious* experience is shaped by his prior personal and social experience, from the birth of his mother, through the death of his father, to the early revealing encounter with his English teacher. There is indeed an "admirable congruity" between the message that Malcolm receives from his brother Reginald about the Nation of Islam and the structure of Malcolm's mind at that point, but that is not to be seen as some happy coincidence. As Proudfoot puts it, "beliefs eventually satisfy adherents because they make sense of an activity to which they have already committed themselves and for which they have as yet insufficient justification."[99] Malcolm's encounter with Islam as preached by Elijah Muhammad introduced him to a much more coherent and extensive justification for his analysis of the plight of the black person in a white society.

So it is also with Malcolm's "second conversion." Malcolm had already largely detached himself from the nation of Islam, and hence from the social reinforcement of its teachings, on account of Elijah Muhammad's shocking transgressions. The vicious response to Malcolm by the Nation of Islam, including the threats of death, was fresh in his mind when he began the pilgrimage to Mecca. In that context, the intense experience of brotherhood with fellow Muslims stood out in sharp relief against Malcolm's recent difficulties. The daily reinforcement of that brotherhood throughout the course of the pilgrimage provided Malcolm with the necessary social support for a change of mind about the inherent evil of the white man. The ritual context encourages Malcolm to interpret his change of mind and his increased fellow-feeling as religious experiences; they thus constitute the core of his second conversion. In neither case can Malcolm's conversion be treated as independent of his prior beliefs and practices or of his immediate and secondary contexts. Proudfoot's critique of James' understanding of religious experience is sustained again by the examination of *The Autobiography of Malcolm X*.

Conclusions

Proudfoot's work and this chapter's analysis of the conversions of Stephen Bradley and Malcolm X suggest that there is an alternative approach to the description, analysis, and interpretation of religious experience. James' characterization of religion as "the feelings, acts, and experiences of individual men in their solitude" can prove to be misleading if it directs the observer to sever moments of religious experience from their contexts in individuals' lives and to cut off those individual lives from their participation in society and history. Feelings, acts, and experiences prior to the moment of religious conversion exert a powerful influence on how that experience is understood, described, and explained. Moreover, it is extraordinarily difficult, and quite likely misleading, to isolate "individual men in their solitude" and thereby to ignore the effects of their social circumstances. Stephen Bradley, for example, had attended a revival just before his experience of the Holy Spirit. He may have been alone at the time, but his immediately prior experience is surely relevant. Various beliefs, practices, and aspects of community organization clearly set the stage for both his experience of conversion and for his understanding of that experience. In his conversion story Malcolm X himself focuses on the prior circumstances that shaped his conversion. He refuses to treat his own experience in isolation; he insists particularly on relating it to that of all black people. The shape and specific concerns of the *Autobiography* do not fit the pattern of conversion described by James in *The Varieties*.

Both Proudfoot's theoretical questions and the evidence of Malcolm X's *Autobiography* thus pose problems for James' understanding of conversion and his general theory of religion. Those problems concern two major areas. First, James selects his examples of conversion from a relatively narrow range; his converts are overwhelmingly Christian and largely Protestant. General theoretical statements about conversion and religion need to have a broader empirical base. To know one religious tradition is not to know them all. James' analytical statements sometimes reveal interesting aspects of the examples he considers, but they do not provide a sufficiently firm basis for the broad statements that he wishes to make. Second, and more importantly, James' theory of religion rules out from the beginning factors that converts themselves (if Malcolm X is any indication) may consider crucial to their conversion. While James' approach is internally consistent, it produces a view of religion that dismisses all too quickly many dimensions of the religious life that religious people, not to mention other theorists, find crucial. Because of its difficulty with sources outside the Christian tradition and because of its theoretical problems and limitations, James' work cannot be considered an adequate general treatment of conversion.

Even if *The Varieties* can not be judged to be wholly successful—though it does contain a number of acute and challenging observations—it has served to raise some important questions about how conversion should be studied. James' focus on the individual brought the topic of religious experience to the fore. Proudfoot's analysis of conversion stories showed that they cannot be perceived as unvarnished representations of immediate experience. Converts themselves are always actively involved in interpreting their own experience, and the stories they tell reflect those interpretations. In the next chapter I will abandon what I see as the problematic attempt to recover the immediate religious experience of converts and concentrate instead on the interpretations of experience that their accounts reveal. In subsequent chapters, I will move beyond the personal context to the broader social and historical contexts in which conversion might be interpreted.

Chapter 2

Augustine of Hippo, Karl Barth, and the Theology of Conversion

In the previous chapter, relying on Proudfoot's analysis of religious experience, I developed a critique of James' conception of religious experience, his understanding of conversion, and his general theory of religion. With Proudfoot, I argued that there is no uninterpreted religious experience, since the very description of an experience as *religious* carries with it an "embedded claim" about its cause and origin.[100] Such claims are, for example, clearly present in Stephen Bradley's and Malcolm X's accounts of their conversions. After describing the racing of his heart and other physical sensations, Bradley quickly attributes them to their specific cause, the activity of the Christian Holy Spirit.[101] No alternatives to that inference are entertained; it is simply stated as a matter of fact, as a part of the description of his experience. Where James would see evidence of a certain type of *experience*, Proudfoot would see an *explanation* of that experience. It will be helpful at this point to distinguish more clearly the processes of description and explanation.

Again, Proudfoot's way of stating the issue is illuminating:

> An emotion, practice, or experience must be described in terms that can plausibly be attributed to the subject on the basis of the available evidence. The subject's self-ascription is normative for describing the experience. This is a kind of first-person privilege that has nothing to do with immediate intuitive access to mental

39

states versus mediated inferential reasoning. It is simply a matter of intentionality[102]

Thus, to ignore or dismiss out of hand Bradley's attribution of his physical symptoms to the Christian Holy Spirit would be to describe his experience inaccurately. To describe his experience accurately, however, does not necessarily require that the observer accept Bradley's interpretation of it. As Proudfoot explains:

> The explanation the analyst offers of that same experience is another matter altogether. It need not be couched in terms familiar or acceptable to the subject. It must be an explanation of the experience as identified under the subject's description, but the subject's approval of the explanation is not required. Bradley's experience might be explained in terms of the conflicts of early adolescence. . . .

> No reference need be made to God or Christ in the construction of these explanations. If the explanation is challenged, the one who proposed it is responsible for providing reasons to support it and for showing how it accounts for the evidence better than any of its rivals does.[103]

Explanations express the interpreter's point of view, convictions about what is important and what is less so, and commitment to a particular theoretical approach. There is no prior requirement of agreement or disagreement with the subject's point of view. While James, Proudfoot, and Bradley himself all need to develop a description of Bradley's experience that could plausibly be accepted by Bradley himself in order to certify that they are, in fact, discussing the same thing, once they have arrived at a such a plausible description of the experience, they are free to differ in their explanations of it. Such specific explanations will typically be dependent upon and indicative of a commitment to a broader scheme of explanation, such as James' theory of religion or Bradley's Christian faith.

Since converts' accounts of their experience include, explicitly or implicitly, their own explanations of their experience, it is necessary to consider those interpretations on their own terms. As Bradley's account suggests, converts' explanations of religious conversion will most often be set forth in explicitly theological terms. The Christian Holy Spirit causes Bradley's physical unrest and also grants him the vision of the New Testament passage that brings him peace. Similarly, Malcolm X records how he understands Allah to have been guiding his life from his youth on.[104] As Malcolm puts it when he fortuitously escapes a confrontation on the streets that likely would have meant death for him or his pursuer: "They say that God takes care of fools and babies. I've so often thought that Allah was watching over me."[105] Such comments constitute *primary* explanations; that is, explanations offered by subjects of their own experience. They are generally partial, ad hoc, and unsystematic, woven into the fabric of the description of the experience and resting on largely implicit assumptions about human beings, the divine, and the like. They express a theology of conversion that is immediate to the experience and not fully elaborated into a complete theological system. Whatever their other virtues, neither Malcolm X nor Stephen Bradley proves himself to be a strikingly original theological thinker in his explanation of his own conversion.

Such primary explanations can, however, reflect the influence of or serve as the basis for *secondary* explanations, intentionally formulated by professional theologians in the tradition in question or even by others outside the tradition. Thus, Bradley's account is likely to have been shaped by the understanding of conversion of Methodist revivals and it could also serve as grist for the mill of any revivalist theologian trying to develop a general theological understanding of the process of conversion. Similarly, in his own preaching and missionary work Malcolm X began to develop and extend the exemplary force of his own conversion.[106] While primary explanations of conversion represent the "embedded claims" about causation that come with any report of experience, secondary explanations represent the considered attempts of individuals, communities, and traditions to extend the usefulness of conversion by incorporating it into ever broader contexts of significance. Secondary explanations of conversion are not less important than primary ones, but they are typically more distanced from the experience in question. As second order explanations, they tend to identify generalized patterns rather than dwell on individual instances. The distinction between primary and secondary explanations is not the same as that between an insider's and an outsider's explanation, since converts' explanations of their own experiences can be incorporated into both forms.

Augustine's Conversion

Primary explanations of conversion in testimonies like those of Stephen Bradley and Malcolm X offer little in the way of sophisticated theological thinking. On occasion, however, particularly in extended autobiographies, they can achieve considerable subtlety and scope. A classic example of such a text in the Christian tradition is the *Confessions* of Augustine of Hippo. Written at the end of the fourth century when Augustine had just assumed the position of bishop in Hippo in North Africa, the *Confessions* review with relentless introspection and disarming appearance of honesty an array of episodes in a life that stretches from Augustine's birth in 354 to his conversion in the summer of 386 and the death of his mother in the late Spring of 387.[107]

Augustine's life, more than that of Malcolm X, was punctuated by an extended series of conversions. At the age of 19 on reading Cicero's *Hortensius*, he converted to the study of philosophy: "I was not encouraged by this work of Cicero's to join this or that sect; instead I was urged on and inflamed with a passionate zeal to love and seek and obtain and embrace and hold fast wisdom itself, whatever it might be."[108] Soon thereafter Augustine turned to the Manichaeans[109] and remained with them as a "hearer" for nine years.[110] Augustine gradually disengaged himself from the Manichees for a variety of reasons[111] and entered, with many doubts yet to be resolved, the Catholic catechumenate.[112] While still pondering his theological and philosophical uncertainties, Augustine chanced upon the writings of a number of Platonists,[113] which did much to resolve his confusion. Yet Augustine's conversion to Catholic Christianity still remained to be accomplished at that point; the *Confessions* recounts the climax of that transformation in book VIII.

The primary explanation of the cause of Augustine's conversion in the *Confessions* is never kept from view. From its opening sentence the text takes the form of an extended hymn or prayer of thanksgiving; it is addressed directly to the God to whom Augustine attributes his salvation. Augustine consistently depicts himself as the passive recipient of God's direction. In the climactic book VIII, for example, he recalls that God led him to the elderly Christian Simplicianus, who told him of the conversion of the famous rhetorician Victorinus.[114] God next moved Augustine to self-scrutiny through a story that Pontitianus told about two comrades of his who had become Christians after reading about the life of St. Antony.[115] Finally, God enabled Augustine to overcome the paralysis of will that kept him from consummating his conversion in the garden at Milan.[116] Augustine makes his attribution of cause quite clear: "For you converted me to you in such a way that I no longer sought a wife nor any other worldly hope."[117]

In order to develop a fuller understanding of Augustine's conversion and his own explanation of it, it will be helpful to examine in greater detail a few of the incidents he recounts. One famous escapade from Augustine's youth (he was sixteen at the time) clearly displays his retrospective view of his pre-conversion self:

> Near our vineyard there was a pear tree, loaded with fruit, though the fruit was not particularly attractive in either color or taste. I and some other wretched youths conceived the idea of shaking the pears off this tree and carrying them away. We set out late at night (having, as we usually did in our depraved way, gone on playing in the streets till that hour) and stole all the fruit that we could carry. And this was not to feed ourselves; we may have tasted a few, but then we threw the rest to the pigs. Our real pleasure was simply in doing something that was not allowed. Such was my heart, God, such was my heart which you had pity on when it was at the very bottom of the abyss. And now let my heart tell you what it was looking for there, that I became evil for nothing, with nor reason for wrongdoing except the wrongdoing itself. The evil was foul, and I loved it; I loved destroying myself; I loved my sin—not the thing for which I had committed the sin, but the sin itself. How base a soul, falling back from your firmament to sheer destruction, not seeking some object by shameful means, but seeking shame for itself.[118]

Unlike Malcolm Little, Augustine did not steal to stave off a persistent hunger; he did it purely for the thrill.[119] The sheer adolescent joy of his action still lurks beneath his sober adult shame. Again unlike Malcolm, Augustine locates the problem demonstrated in his theft not in external circumstances, but in his own internal disposition. Where Malcolm sought "help" for a problem of massive social and historical dimensions, Augustine seeks a cure for the maladies of the individual human soul. Augustine has identified no less recalcitrant a problem but it is one with an entirely different personal, social, and historical location. Throughout his narrative Malcolm maintains an impressively strong sense of self; throughout his, Augustine lays bare the agonies of a self continuously open to revision and suffering doubt. James, not surprisingly, introduces Augustine as a classic example of a "discordant personality, with melancholy in the form of self-condemnation and sense of sin."[120] A sense of sin and the problem of evil dog Augustine throughout his life. Those concerns weave in and out of his restless quest for wisdom and find their resolution only in his final conversion to Catholic Christianity.

As Augustine remembers it, sinfulness marked even his earliest actions: "Even in my infancy . . . I was doing something that deserved blame."[121] Little changes as Augustine begins his formal education: "We sinned by doing less than was demanded of us in writing or reading or studying literature."[122] Throughout his boyhood, Augustine's "sin was in this—that I looked for pleasures, exaltations, truths not in God Himself but in His creatures (myself and the rest), and so I fell straight into sorrows, confusions, and mistakes."[123] The young man's awakening sexuality opened an entirely new area for transgression. Yet even "when, in fact, I had not committed a sin that would put me on a level with the worst sinners, I used to pretend that I had committed it, so that I might not be despised for my greater degree of innocence or thought less of for a comparative chastity."[124] Even when Augustine progresses in his study of philosophy and his career as a rhetorician, he is hounded by the same feelings: "And what good did it do me that I, at a time when I was the vile slave of evil desires, read and understood for myself every book that I could lay my hands on which dealt with what are called the liberal arts?"[125]

Though it seems to have played no explicit role in Augustine's initial conversion to philosophy, his quest for the origin of evil does seem to have moved Augustine to begin his association with the Manichees, soon thereafter. Despite other difficulties which he had within the community, the Manichaean view of evil maintained a powerful sway over Augustine, as is evident in his description of his state of mind in Rome. Prior to his trip to Rome in 383, Augustine's long-anticipated meeting with the Manichaean leader Faustus had left him sadly disappointed: "I lost the enthusiasm which I had

had for the writings of Manes [Mani], and I had all the less confidence in the other Manichaean teachers after I found that the famous Faustus had shown up so badly in many of the questions which perplexed me."[126] Faustus' poor intellectual performance led Augustine to forsake whatever ambition he had "to go far in that sect,"[127] though it did not cause him immediately to sever his ties with the Manichaeans. His disengagement from the Manichees, or his conversion out of the group, took place gradually. It was aided by his decision to leave Carthage for Rome, there to pursue further his career in rhetoric. While recovering from an illness contracted in Rome, Augustine considered his current, Manichaean, solution to his perennial problem:

> For I was still of the opinion that it is not we
> ourselves who sin, but some other nature which
> is in us; it gratified my pride to think that I
> was blameless and, if I did something wrong,
> not to confess that I had done it, so that you
> [God] might heal my soul, because my soul had
> sinned against you. Instead I like to excuse
> myself and accuse something else—something
> that was in me but was not really I. But in
> fact I was wholly I and it was my impiety that
> divided one me from another me. My sin was
> all the more incurable because I imagined that
> I was not a sinner. . . .[128]

In Augustine's understanding, the Manichaean conception of the universe as divided between the powers of Light and the powers of Darkness absolves him of any personal responsibility for wrongdoing. Since his true identity is as a son of the Light which is good, any evil must be caused by "some other nature which is in us." Though the individual may be seen as the battleground of the warring forces of Light and Darkness, the effects of either power are beyond personal control. Wrongdoing thus is not a matter of the human will, but rather a part of a cosmic drama played out on an individual scale. That understanding of the nature of evil proves difficult indeed for Augustine to shake.

Even when Augustine makes a forthright, if tentative, external commitment to the Christian community—"I shall take my stand where my parents placed me as a child until I can see the truth plainly"[129]—he remains vexed by the problem of evil: "I still could not understand clearly and distinctly what was the cause of evil."[130] Through his reading and thinking Augustine eventually concludes that the Manichees' depiction of evil is not convincing, but he cannot develop a satisfactory alternative. As he explains his struggle:

> And I made an effort to understand what I had heard [in Christian circles], that free will is the cause of our doing evil and your [God's] just judgment the cause of our suffering it; but I could not grasp this clearly. And so, though I tried to raise the eyes of my mind from the pit, I fell back into it again and as often as I tried so often did I fall back. But I was a little raised up toward your light by the fact that I was just as certain that I had a will as that I had a life. So when I willed to do or not to do something, I was perfectly certain that the act of willing was mine and not anybody else's, and I was not getting near to the conclusion that here was the cause of my sin.[131]

Augustine's abandonment of the Manichaeans' external and impersonal characterization of evil for an internal and personal one represents a major change in his thinking, but one whose implications still remain to be solidly grasped by him. Its full impact on Augustine comes later when, with the aid of the writings of certain Platonist philosophers,[132] he jettisons the notion that evil is in any way material. As Augustine puts it, "All things that are, are good, and as to that evil, the origin of which I was seeking for, it is not a substance, since, if it were a substance, it would be good."[133] That chain of reasoning leads Augustine to his final characterization of evil:

> . . . it is not a substance but a perversity of the will turning away from you, God, the supreme substance, toward lower things—casting away, as it were, its own insides, and swelling with desire for what is outside it.[134]

With that, Augustine seems at last to have a satisfactory intellectual solution to the origin and nature of evil. In itself, however, that philosophical and theological resolution is not sufficient to effect his conversion.

Several other strands of Augustine's thought and activity reach their culmination in his conversion to Catholic Christianity. After his initial encounter with Cicero, Augustine was "inflamed with a passionate zeal to love and seek and obtain and embrace and hold fast wisdom itself."[135] He had the intellectual's natural predilection to find that wisdom in books. Immediately after his first philosophical conversion, Augustine had tried, and found wanting, the Christian scriptures. They simply seemed "unworthy of comparison with the grand style of Cicero."[136] Neither the writings of the Manichees nor his dabbling in astrology could satisfy Augustine's intellectual demands.[137] Yet it was not until Augustine heard scriptural sermons by Ambrose of Milan that he could take the Christian scriptures seriously. Through his eloquence and intellect, Ambrose offered an alternative interpretation of texts that Augustine had formerly despised:

> . . . especially when I had heard one or two passages in the Old Testament explained, usually in a figurative way, which, when I had taken them literally, had been a cause of death to me. So, after a number of these passages had been explained to me in their spiritual sense, I began to blame that despairing attitude of mine which had led me to believe that the Law and the Prophets could not possibly stand up to hostile and mocking criticism.[138]

Peter Brown suggests that even though it is largely hidden from view, "the influence of Ambrose on Augustine is far out of proportion to any direct contact which the two men may have had."[139] Augustine later acknowledged that his confidence had been shaken after his unsatisfactory meeting with Faustus and his departures from the Manichaean community in North Africa and then the community in Rome. He met Ambrose at a time when his certainties about the sources of wisdom and his solutions for the problem of evil had been cast into doubt. While Ambrose's exegesis of scripture has shown Augustine the possibility of a sophisticated and philosophically legitimate interpretation of the biblical texts, it remains for him only a beginning of a new intellectual path. Augustine expresses the goal of his quest in characteristic fashion:

> We must look into things more carefully and not give up hope. And now see, those things in the Scriptures which used to seem absurd are not absurd; they can be understood in a different and perfectly good way. I shall take my stand where my parents placed me as a child until I can see the truth plainly. But where shall I look for it? And when shall I look for it? Ambrose has no spare time; nor have I time for reading. *And where can I find the books?*[140]

The books that Augustine finds, eventually, are those of certain Neoplatonist philosophers.[141] They taught him "to seek for a truth which was incorporeal"[142] and offered him a way of understanding the nature and origin of evil that resolved his previous doubts. Augustine confesses that he is convinced that "you [God] wanted me to come upon these books before I made a study of your Scriptures,"[143] since they furnish him with the proper philosophical perspective for unlocking the hidden truths of scripture. When he begins with the writings of the apostle Paul, Augustine finds that "everything in the Platonists which I had found true was expressed here, but it was expressed to the glory of your grace."[144]

Augustine thus approaches the climactic events of his life having achieved considerable intellectual certainty about the questions that had occupied him most. In both cases his encounter with neo-Platonic philosophy had been crucial. On the one hand, it gave him a way of (re-)conceiving the nature of God and the world, and hence evil. On the other, it provided him with the intellectual tools to develop a philosophically sophisticated reading of scripture and thus to overcome its superficial crudities and difficulties. His reading of the Platonists brings to an apparent climax the quest for wisdom that had begun at least with his reading of Cicero's *Hortensius* and the meditation on evil which he traces in retrospect to the earliest days of his life. There is a sense, a very real sense,[145] in which Augustine is converted again with his acceptance of the Platonists' work. Yet the nature of that conversion and the question of its relationship to the climax of Augustine's conversion as recounted in the *Confessions* need to be investigated further. Consider Augustine's exposition of it in a text written in the autumn of 386:

> We never ceased to sigh for Philosophy, and thought of nothing but of that form of life which we had agreed to live among ourselves. . . . Suddenly some substantial books appeared . . . and sprinkled on this little flame a few small drops of precious ointment. They started up an incredible blaze, incredible, Romanianus, quite incredible, more than you might perhaps believe if I told you. What can I say? It was more powerful than I, myself, can bring myself to believe. After this how could honour, human pomp, desire for empty fame, the consolations and attractions of this

dying life, move me. Swiftly, I turned in upon
myself.[146]

Without any designation of the author, such a text might
well be taken as an example of conversion to philosophy
in Late Antiquity. There is no explicit mention of a god,
let alone of the specifically Christian belief in Jesus as
the Christ. Nor is there any mention of the Christian
scriptures, unless they could be identified with the
"substantial books" that started the philosophical fire.
That passionate expression of enthusiasm is spoken in a
voice distinctly different from that of the *Confessions*. As
such, it helps to bring into sharp relief the specific
primary explanation of his own conversion that Augustine proposes in his *Confessions*. The various elements of
that explanation are all on display in the eighth book,
which leads the reader up to and through the climactic
scene in the garden at Milan.

The opening passage makes it clear that Augustine
does not conceive of his conversion as a matter of his
own intellectual assent to philosophical and theological
doctrines:

> My God, let me remember with thanks and let
> me confess to you your mercies done to
> me. . . . I will tell how it was that you broke
> my bonds, and all your worshippers who hear
> this will say: "Blessed be the Lord in heaven
> and in earth, great and wonderful is His
> name."[147]

Augustine actually proceeds on two tracks in book VIII,
as he does in the rest of the *Confessions*. On the one
hand, he provides in his description of his experience
ample material for a variety of explanations of it. The
sheer bulk of the various modern psychological, sociological, historical, religious, and theological interpretations
of Augustine's conversion is truly impressive.[148] On the
other hand, descriptions of experience being what they
are, Augustine explains precisely how he wants his
conversion to be understood. I will focus on how
Augustine provides a clear and full explanation of his
conversion as a saving act of God. To appreciate fully
Augustine's "embedded claim" about the nature and
origin of his experience, it will be helpful to consider the
description he provides in book VIII of the *Confessions*
in greater detail.

In book VIII Augustine relates a series of scenes that
dramatize the impact that stories about the conversions
of other people have had on him. Those vignettes play a

prominent role in his description of his own experience, without becoming the only explanation of it. In chapter two the elderly Christian Simplicianus, to whom Augustine considers himself led by God, begins an account of the conversion to Christianity of the rhetor Victorinus. As Augustine recalls, Simplicianus' motives were transparent; he intended "to lead me toward the humility of Christ."[149] Explaining that it is a story which reveals the action of God's grace, Augustine retells at some length what Simplicianus had told him about Victorinus' success as a scholar, his thorough scrutiny of the Christian scriptures, his private resolve to become a Christian, and his sudden and unexpected decision to receive baptism publicly. The story about Victorinus' conversion provokes in Augustine a meditation on the joy that attends the salvation of those in very great danger. It concludes with the plea: "*Come, Lord, act upon us*: rouse us up and call us back!"[150] The emphasis on God as the agent of conversion is insistent.

Eventually, Augustine confesses the impact which the story had on him: "When this man of yours, Simplicianus, told me all this about Victorinus, I was on fire to be like him, and this, of course, was why he had told me the story."[151] It is important for an understanding of Augustine's explanation of his own experience, however, that he does not attribute the unfolding events either to his own human initiative or to the personal influence of the story-teller; rather, Simplicianus is the vehicle of God's will for Augustine.

Simplicianus certainly had described a model which Augustine could imitate in his own conversion to Christianity. The timing, details, structure, and rhetoric of the story are remembered by Augustine as being carefully orchestrated in order to encourage him to adopt a certain course of action. The conversion of Victorinus is presented not as a matter for disinterested consideration but as a challenge that seeks a response. Clearly, the praise for Victorinus' impressive learning and his courage in the profession of his new faith is designed to spur Augustine on. Simplicianus presents conversion to Christianity as an intellectual process, founded on thorough study and deep meditation.[152] Commitment to Christianity is also portrayed as a public action which must persist in the face of opposition from friends and associates and which must overcome vanity and self-doubt. In Christianity, Simplicianus implicitly argues, Augustine can imitate both the intellectual depth and the moral courage of Victorinus. But Augustine consistently sees behind the evident craft of Simplicianus' story a grander design. About the story of Victorinus' conversion, Augustine writes: "It is a story which ought to be confessed to you [God], containing, as it does, great praise of your grace."[153] Like the nameless individual in "Amazing Grace," Augustine sees God's grace at work in human events. The story of Victorinus' conversion provokes Augustine to wonder: "By what means did you [God] find your way into that man's heart?"[154] As James writes, "In the religion of the twice-born . . . the world is a double-storied mystery."[155] Augustine looks beyond the persuasive efforts of a crafty story-teller and the attractive example of someone both similar to and more accomplished than himself for a deeper, more mysterious—more amazing—meaning. In each of the episodes of book VIII Augustine sees the hand of God.

Soon after Augustine's meditation on the example of Victorinus, he describes his encounter with Ponticianus, a fellow-countryman and an official at the imperial court. When Pontitianus finds that Augustine has been reading the scriptures, he begins a conversation about the Egyptian monk Antony. That quickly leads to Ponticianus' account of how two friends of his, on reading the *Life of Antony*, turned to lives of asceticism. Again, Augustine recalls that the example had a profound and unsettling effect: "But you, Lord, while he was speaking, were turning me around so that I could see myself; you took me from behind my own back, which was where I had put myself during the time when I did not want to be observed by myself, and you set me in front of my own face so that I could see how foul a sight I was."[156] After other similar comments Augustine draws an explicit comparison: "But now the more ardent was the love I felt for those two men of whom I was hearing and of how healthfully they had been moved to give themselves up entirely to be cured, the more bitter was the hatred I felt for myself when I compared myself with them."[157] In those remarks Augustine does provide a vivid description of his inner state, but it cannot be divorced from his perception that God is acting upon him through the medium of Ponticianus' story.

That story even leads Augustine to remember his youthful conversion to philosophy and the time that he had spent as a Manichee. It prompts a review of his spiritual and intellectual life up to that point. Augustine finds, to his anguish, that he suffers greatly in comparison to Ponticianus' friends. He asks his ever-present companion Alypius: "Is it because they have gone ahead that we are ashamed to follow? And do we feel no shame at not even following at all?"[158] Yet, as the rest of his narrative makes clear, Augustine claims that he was powerless, in himself, to act on the example in the story.

Again, in the case of Ponticianus, the conversion story is clearly told to commend the example of the two anonymous friends, the example of Antony, and the power of the scriptures. The emphasis shifts from intellectual investigation and moral courage to the acceptance of messages found, quite by accident, in books, a phenomenon which finds deep resonance in Augustine's intellectual life. The impact which the gospel according to Matthew had upon Antony and which the *Life of Antony* had upon Ponticianus' two friends both anticipate the effect which a random reading of a passage from Paul's letter to the Romans will soon have on Augustine. Augustine's comments throughout chapters seven and eight of book VIII show that he took Ponticianus' story deeply to heart. Augustine sees God acting on him through the story as he compares himself to the two converts. Like that of Simplicianus, Ponticianus' story is not completely successful in provoking Augustine's conversion, but Augustine remembers it as moving him closer to that goal.

The acknowledged but limited success of those stories can best be understood in relation to the theological conviction that dominates the *Confessions*: Augustine's conversion is accomplished by God, not by his own human efforts or those of any others. Augustine simply refuses to portray social interaction with Simplicianus and Pontitianus or his own intellectual consideration of their stories as in themselves decisive influences on his own conversion. He does not describe his own conversion as in any way volitional; despite his efforts, Augustine's conversion can only occur when he surrenders himself to God. He consistently emphasizes his own inability to effect his self-transformation and attributes it instead to the activity of God. As Augustine recalls the events in the garden, he was virtually powerless to bring about the final stage of his conversion through his own efforts:

> I was saying inside myself: "Now, now let it be now!" and as I spoke the words I was already beginning to go in the direction I wanted to go. I nearly managed it, but I did not quite manage it. Yet I did not slip right back to the

beginning; I was a stage above that, and I stood
there to regain my breath. And I tried again
and I was very nearly there; I was almost
touching it and grasping it, and then I was not
there, I was not touching it, I was not grasping
it; I hesitated to die to death and live to life;
inveterate evil had more power over me than
the novelty of good, and as that very moment
in time in which I was to become something
else drew nearer and nearer, it struck me with
more and more horror. But I was not struck
right back or turned aside; I was just held in
suspense.[159]

In terms that bring back to mind James' discussion of
the divided self, Augustine summarizes his situation: "So
went the controversy in my heart—about self, and self
against self."[160] Augustine then drags himself off to a
garden, wracked by tears and wondering if his torment
will be resolved. It takes divine intervention, in the form
of a child's voice, to turn Augustine completely around:

Suddenly a voice reaches my ears from a
nearby house. It is the voice of a boy or a girl
(I don't know which) and in a kind of singsong
the words are constantly repeated: "Take it and
read it. Take it and read it." At once my face
changed, and I began to think carefully of
whether the singing of words like these came
into any kind of game which children play, and
I could not remember that I had heard
anything like it before.[161]

Like Stephen Bradley, with the racing of his heart and
other physical symptoms, Augustine quickly moves to
attribute his experience to the proper cause:

I checked the force of my tears and rose to my
feet, being quite certain that *I must interpret
this as a divine command* to me to open the
book and read the first passage which I should
come upon.[162]

Again like Bradley, Augustine is directed to the New
Testament, to the letter of Paul to the Romans:

I snatched up the book, opened it, and read in
silence the passage upon which my eyes first
fell: "not in reveling and drunkenness, not in
debauchery and licentiousness, not in quarrel-
ling and jealousy. But put on the Lord Jesus
Jesus Christ, and make no provision for the

flesh, to gratify its desires." I had no wish to read further; there was no need to. For immediately I had reached the end of this sentence it was as though my heart was filled with a light of confidence and all the shadows of my doubt were swept away.[163]

Like Bradley, Augustine recalls that an overwhelming sense of contentment suffused his soul with the unification of his divided self. God has converted Augustine and brought him peace.

As he has throughout his narrative, Augustine reserves the decisive role in his conversion for God himself. He summarizes that explanation at the close of book VIII: "For you converted me to in such a way that I no longer sought a wife nor any other worldly hope."[164] In doing that, he is no different than Stephen Bradley, who explained his own conversion as the action of the Christian Holy Spirit, or Malcolm X, who saw in his whole life the guidance of Allah. Augustine is quite willing to observe that God can act through the examples of others, as he explicitly mentions at several points in book VIII, but he wants to avoid the misunderstanding that such examples are sufficient in themselves. To interpret them in that way would be to miss the "double-storied mystery" of Augustine's world.

Kenneth Burke captures clearly the intention of Augustine's interpretation of his own experience:

His very stress upon the importance of the will had made him especially sensitive to the fact that a change within had taken place as though from without (or it would be more accurate to say, "as though from more deeply within"). He had done many things, and wanted many things, and wanted not to want many things— but now he had *been* converted. The felt difference in the quality of his motivation must have convinced him that some power beyond him must have turned in order for him to be turned.[165]

Augustine's account of the climax of his conversion sets his adoption of a neo-Platonic understanding of Christianity in an explicitly religious context. To Augustine, his conversion was not something that he willed, but the direct result of God's activity. As Augustine so vividly recalls, his own will was powerless to effect the final transformation. His conversion was most emphatically *something that happened to him* and not something that he himself accomplished. God acts decisively in bringing Augustine to an understanding of the passage from Paul's letter to the Romans as a message personally directed to him. That allows Augustine to re-interpret the meaning of his life from the vantage point of his conversion. His continuing preoccupation with the problem of evil is resolved ultimately not by a shift of intellectual allegiance from the Manicheans to the Platonists but by "putting on the Lord Jesus Christ." His quest for the books that would reveal to him wisdom culminates in the Christian scriptures, more specifically the New Testament and the letters of Paul, particularly the letter to the Romans to which he will later devote a commentary. His own book, the *Confessions*, becomes Augustine's prayer of thanksgiving for God's intervention in his life. Like the testimonies of many converts, it aims to glorify God for his gracious action and to attract the attention, if not the imitation, of those who have not yet committed their lives to a similar path.[166]

Augustine's explanation of his conversion experience introduces ideas about God, sin, and the human will that remain important in Christian theological thought. More than anything else, however, it is his radical insistence that conversion is an *act of God* that will become a prominent feature of later Christian theological thinking about conversion. It surfaces in Roman Catholic as well as Protestant treatments of the topic. As Karl Rahner puts it: "From the biblical and dogmatic point of view, man's free turning to God *has always to be seen* as a response, made possible by God's grace, to a call from God."[167] In Bernard Lonergan's formulation: "Religious conversion is *being grasped by* ultimate concern."[168] Both of those descriptions emphasize that conversion is, and should be, a matter of self-surrender. A proper Christian theological explanation must play down the volitional aspects and stress the dependence of the convert on the grace of God. Perhaps no contemporary Christian theologian has emphasized as strongly and as fruitfully the fundamental importance of God's call to human beings as Karl Barth.

Karl Barth on Conversion

Barth's discussion of conversion is particularly interesting because, like that of James, it clearly depends upon and is indicative of his general theoretical understanding of religion. Barth discusses conversion in the volume of his *Church Dogmatics* devoted to "The Doctrine of Reconciliation" within the chapter treating "Jesus Christ, The Servant as Lord" in the section on "The Sanctification of Man."[169] Barth announces his thesis at the beginning of that section:

> The exaltation of man, which in defiance of his reluctance has been achieved in the death and declared in the resurrection of Jesus Christ, is as such the creation of his new form of existence as the faithful covenant-partner of God. It rests wholly and utterly on his justification before God, and like this it is achieved only in the one Jesus Christ, but effectively and authoritatively in Him.[170]

In that scheme of understanding, "the conversion of man is a decision of God for him which not only makes possible a corresponding decision of man for God, the free act of his obedience, but makes this act and obedience real, directly causing it to take place."[171] The activity of God which Augustine stressed in his account of his own conversion is the cornerstone of Barth's interpretation not only of conversion but also of religion and revelation in general.

Barth incessantly stresses the fact that it is God who converts human beings, not humans who convert themselves.[172] Using the biblical metaphor of sleep, he argues that Christians do not awake of their own accord. Left to their own devices they would remain asleep, even if they were themselves convinced that they were most vitally awake. Indeed, for Barth the volitional aspects of conversion, and of human religious life in general, are primary indicators of the serious problems caused by human attempts to know God. True conversion, Barth will argue, can only come about with total self-surrender. Christians, like James' twice-born souls, should live in a world that is a "double-storied mystery"; it is essential that they recognize that the "divine mystery and miracle of sanctification"[173] is to be found in the activity of God.

From that starting point Barth proceeds to consider several facets of conversion. He does not want his emphasis on the activity of God to obliterate the human dimensions of conversion, so he stresses that the whole being of the human participant is intimately involved in the process. Nonetheless, "the reality of this event depends wholly on the reality of God."[174] Indeed, given his biblical characterization as the author of a covenant of free grace, "God would not be God if this awakening did not take place."[175] God's gracious act of sanctification truly demonstrated his divine nature.

Conversion, for Barth, involves the whole person—the heart, the mind, the will, the disposition, and any subsequent action. Moreover, he conceives conversion to be a *lifelong process*, rather than a momentary event. It appears that Barth would not be willing to understand Stephen Bradley's experience as a conversion, at least without a significant amount of further information. For Barth:

> Momentary events of this kind—. . . in the Pietist or Methodist form of a simple or more complex experience of conversion—are not identical with with conversion to God, because the latter is the totality of the movement of sanctification which dominates and characterises human life—a movement in which there can be no breaks or pauses when conversion is no longer needed or only needed afresh . . . .[176]

Barth's characterization of conversion as a lifelong process differs even from the picture of Augustine's life as being marked by a series of conversions. If a human life can be punctuated by several, distinct conversions, conversion itself must remain a clearly delimited, identifiable process, whether it be short in duration and virtually instantaneous or gradual and prolonged. Barth chooses instead to characterize conversion as *a way of life*; conversion describes the lives of human beings who recognize and believe that God is for them and they are for God. Conversion thus becomes a shorthand designation for the Christian life.

What makes that life possible is the revelation of God. Barth acknowledges that God's revelation in Jesus Christ must be the rock-solid foundation for any understanding of conversion: "The event of revelation which has been our starting-point in all these discussions must be merely the manifestation of a real event which takes place with incontestable objectivity."[177] Jesus Christ, as the climax of God's revelation, enables the conversion of human beings to become real. Even if their conversions pale in comparison to the biblical record, they are ennobled by their participation in Jesus Christ's conversion of them and the world:

> It is in His conversion that we are engaged. It is in His birth, from above, the mystery and miracle of Christmas, that we are born again. It is in His Baptism in Jordan that we are baptised with the Holy Ghost and with fire. It is in His death on the cross that we are dead as old men, and in his resurrection in the garden of Joseph of Arimathea that we are risen as new men.[178]

Barth thus sets the conversion of the individual Christian into a scenario of cosmic significance, centered on the act of justification accomplished by God in Jesus Christ. In addition to insisting, more vigorously even than Augustine, that conversion is the activity of God, Barth extends the moment of conversion to include the entirety of one's life. Conversion becomes not a once-and-for-all event, but a daily struggle. Along with Luther, Barth sees human beings as simultaneously justified and sinners. Consequently, that tension characterizes their conversions and their lives as Christians. Barth rejects dichotomies such as the ones expressed in the first verse of "Amazing Grace." A simple division into lost and found, blind and sighted, does not adequately express the human situation of the convert; it dissolves the lifelong process of conversion into a momentary, and hence completed, experience. In contrast, Barth argues:

> The *vita christiana* in conversion is the event, the act, the history, in which at one and the same time man is still wholly the old man and already wholly the new—so powerful is the sin by which he is determined from behind, and so powerful the grace by which he is determined from before. It is in this way that man knows himself when he is really engaged in conversion.[179]

Conversion is an open-ended process that one engages in; its end lies beyond this life. It is the appropriate response to God's revelation.

As Barth's discussion of conversion is founded on his understanding of revelation, so also is his general conception of religion. For Barth, religion, simply put, is "unbelief."[180] Religion represents the audacious, and necessarily doomed, human attempt to grasp God. As Barth puts it: "From the standpoint of revelation religion is clearly seen to be a human attempt to anticipate what God in His revelation wills to do and does do. It is the attempted replacement of the divine work by a human manufacture."[181] Religion turns a deaf ear to God's revelation, preferring to harken instead to the seductive calls of human artifice. But, Barth argues, human attempts to know God are inevitably futile; true knowledge of God, through revelation, is given by God, not seized by human beings.

All religions, then, including Christianity, insofar as they rely on human effort to attain knowledge of God, are destined to fail and to frustrate their adherents. In contrast, "Revelation encounters man on the presupposition and in confirmation of the fact that man's attempts to know God from his own standpoint are wholly and entirely futile."[182] Since religions, by definition for Barth, ignore God's revelation, they can never, as such, *be* true. He asserts that they can, however, *become* true by the grace of God. Religion is not only judged as unbelief by revelation, it

> can just as well be exalted in revelation, even
> though the judgment still stands. It can be
> upheld by it and concealed in it. It can be
> justified by it, and—we must at once add—
> sanctified. Revelation can adopt religion and
> mark it off as true religion.[183]

Barth's further argument that Christianity is the proper locus of true religion, that it can become true religion, is less important here than another interpretive move that Barth makes. It provides him with a point of entry for describing Christianity as the true religion:

> There is a true religion: *just as there are
> justified sinners*. If we abide strictly by that
> analogy—and we are dealing not merely with
> an analogy, but in a comprehensive sense with
> the thing itself—we need have no hesitation in
> saying that the Christian religion is the true
> religion.[184]

Barth's comparison is the key to his understanding both of religion and of conversion. In strict parallel, a religion can become true and a sinner can become justified. In each instance the emphasis falls on an continual process, an unending struggle. God's revelation challenges human beings, as individuals and in groups, to live out its consequences. Insofar as they do, bearing in mind their feeble approximation to the biblical models, they may become "justified" or "true." But just as the individual in conversion is simultaneously justified and a sinner, so are religions simultaneously true, in so far as they conform to God's revelation, and false, in so far as they rely solely on human aspirations.

As with James, there is a remarkable consistency in Barth's movement from a general consideration of religion to a specific treatment of conversion. Barth's emphasis on the paramount importance of God's revelation never wavers; he consistently depicts human efforts to be reckoned righteous in the eyes of God as eternally inadequate by their very nature. Neither Barth's conception of religion nor his view of conversion is static. In each case the continuing dynamic encounter with God's revelation is determinative. The great danger is the reliance on human initiative, because when that occurs conversion becomes confusion; religion, unbelief. Barth's interpretation of conversion constitutes a secondary explanation of religious experience; it is an attempt to develop a coherent, general picture of what Christian conversion is, and more importantly, *should be*. Unlike Augustine, who bases his primary explanation on his own experience of conversion, Barth takes as his point of departure the biblical record and subsequent meditations on it by thinkers such as Calvin. Barth proceeds less by considering individual cases and more by synthesizing diverse explanations of conversion into a coherent whole. Barth's goal is not only to be descriptive and explanatory, but also normative. He intends to develop a canon against which claims of conversion can be judged. His dismissal of the Pietist or Methodist conversion as "not identical with conversion to God" is a good example.

Conclusions

Barth's theological interpretation of conversion has led the discussion far afield from the question of religious experience. It represents, nonetheless, the logical continuation of Proudfoot's argument that perhaps the most distinctive characteristic of religious experience is its claim to be religious. Since the description of an experience as religious includes an embedded claim about the cause of that experience, those who would study religious experience need to study such claims as well. Moreover, since the embedded explanations assert that a given experience is *religious*, they will take the form of ad hoc theological assertions. Statements about how God has acted in one individual's life imply, at least, some general notions about the nature and activity of God, the nature of human beings, and the purpose of human life. Malcolm X's conviction that Allah was guiding his life from his youth onwards and Stephen Bradley's attribution of his physical symptoms to the Christian Holy Spirit are cases in point. Seen in the same light, Augustine's *Confessions* represents a much more elaborate and conscious working out of the same process. In the *Confessions* the explanatory thesis is hardly embedded; it is thrust upon the reader from the opening line. I have called such explanations of religious experience proposed by the subjects *primary explanations* in order to emphasize their immediate and personal character. They give voice, with greater or less sophistication, to the subject's theological views, even when they are not explicitly, formally, and systematically presented as such. They are most often theology with a small "t;" they are more like the "theology' of a Stephen Bradley or a Malcolm X than that of a Karl Barth. But whatever sort of theology they might be, they lead directly to a consideration of more formal theological understandings of conversion. In turn, whatever their relation to their authors' personal religious experience, those theologies characteristically take the form of secondary explanations, based to a very large extent on the experience of others. Their goal is systematization, generalization, and, as is proper for theology, the setting of norms. They take as their subject matter not the conversion of Augustine or Stephen Bradley or the author at hand, but the whole field of Christian conversion, or Muslim conversion, or conversion in whatever religious tradition the theologian stands. Their interest is not so much in the variety of religious experience, but in its underlying unity. They strive less to describe what did happen to a given person and more to prescribe what should happen to any convert worthy of the designation.

In some ways the concern with prescribing norms is peculiar to the theological enterprise and will be left behind with this chapter. Explanations of conversion can be developed from a variety of perspectives; theology is only one of them. Theological explanations focus on the interaction between the divine and the human individual as the interpretive key. Sociological explanations, by contrast, focus on the social circumstances and interpersonal relationships of the convert in question. The following chapters will consider explanatory approaches to the topic of religious conversion which move beyond the personal, psychological, and theological to the sociological and historical.

The Unification Church and the Sociology of Conversion

Peter Berger and Thomas Luckmann direct attention to the social context of conversion and minimize the importance of the conversion experience *per se*:

> To have a conversion experience is nothing much. The real thing is to be able to keep on taking it seriously; to retain a sense of its plausibility. *This* is where the religious community comes in.[185]

Their formulation of the issue explicitly reverses the emphasis of William James. Where James saw the religious community to be a "second-hand" phenomenon, Berger and Luckmann stress the crucial role of the social group in validating, nurturing, extending, and defining the meaning of that experience. Taking an example from the earliest history of Christianity, they contend

> Saul may have become Paul in the aloneness of religious ecstasy, but he could *remain* Paul only in the context of the Christian community that recognized him as such and confirmed the "new being" in which he now located this identity.[186]

As that example suggests, the study of the social context of conversion can take its material from diverse times and places. Much of the most interesting and influential work, however, has been based on the observation of new religious movements in North America and Europe, particularly in the United States.

From a certain perspective, the rise of new religions in the last three decades in the United States is hardly a novelty. As Rodney Stark and William Sims Bainbridge claim in their thorough overview of the current religious scene: "In the beginning all religions are obscure, tiny, deviant cult movements."[187] Nevertheless, contemporary "cults,"[188] including the Holy Spirit Association for the Unification of World Christianity (the Unification Church or "Moonies"), the International Society for Krishna Consciousness ("Hare Krishnas"), the followers of Bhagwan Shree Rajneesh ("Rajneeshis") and many others, have elicited a flood of literature, both in scholarly circles and the popular press. Spectacular public battles over "deprogramming" (which its opponents in some new religious movements prefer to call "faith breaking"), alleged instances of kidnapping by both partisans and opponents of the new religions, and parental requests that the courts grant them temporary conservatorships over their young adult children have created plenty of friction and heat but not always an equal amount of intellectual light. Much of the concern about cults and conversion in modern America has focused on Sun Myung Moon's Unification Church.

Conversion and Deprogramming

Founded in Korea in 1954, Moon's movement made rather desultory progress in this country until the Reverend Moon himself set up a permanent residence in the United States in 1971.[189] Fueled by his presence and the extraordinary missionary efforts of early members, the movement grew significantly in the early seventies. That growth attracted increased scholarly and public attention. To a great extent, both groups focused on the topic of conversion. Based on memoirs of ex-members with titles like *Crazy for God* and *Hostage to Heaven*, the popularization of psychiatric studies of thought reform in prisoner of war camps, and the chilling testimonies of parents about the radical transformations suffered by their children, various advocacy groups and the popular press developed a view of conversion to new religious movements, including the Unification Church, as a form of "brainwashing." "Cult" members were portrayed as having been "programmed" by venal and opportunistic leaders; they could be brought back to normalcy only by a process of "deprogramming." The urgent stories of the popular and influential deprogrammer, Ted Patrick, furnish particularly vivid examples of that kind of reasoning. In his view:

> The way they get them is by on-the-spot hypnosis. Once they get them, they brainwash them. The technique is the same as the North Koreans used on our prisoners of war. . . .

> They don't let a kid sleep, they don't let him eat. They hit him with tape recordings of Scripture, lectures, discussions, workshops—night and day. They wear him down, wear him out. Pretty soon he believes anything. Some kids go out fundraising three days after they join.[190]

After the initial encounter, Patrick claims, cult members are so thoroughly "programmed" that there is "no longer any question of their exercising anything that could reasonably be called free will."[191] Accordingly, cult members cannot exit of their own free will; they have to be led back to reality. But the process, according to Patrick, has its intrinsic rewards:

> After two days of talking, with three of us taking turns, she suddenly gave in. She snapped, just as if someone had turned on a light inside her. The change in her appearance, her expression, her eyes—it was startling. I was amazed. It was like seeing someone return from the grave. It was the most beautiful thing I'd ever seen.[192]

So strong is Patrick's belief in the need for deprogramming that he is more than willing to break the law to accomplish his mission.[193] Patrick's position, however, is not strictly representative of all deprogrammers. Some have shunned the term altogether because of its association with bullying tactics and prefer to style themselves "exit counselors." Nevertheless, Patrick's comments display in an exaggerated but particularly vivid form the inner logic of deprogramming and associated activities, specifically the operative assumptions about human behavior and responsibility.

Deprogramming shares with the Christian theological understanding of conversion a fundamental tenet: the image of the passive self, incapable through its own efforts of attaining the desired goal. Just as Augustine found himself, despite the strenuous efforts of his will, unable to complete his own conversion and Barth stressed that any attempts to know God by relying solely on human effort could never achieve of themselves their stated goal, so also do the partisans of deprogramming (practitioners, parents, and sucessful subjects) insist that the desired transformation is beyond the cult member's power. Those who join new religious movements are consistently pictured as passive dupes who are manipulated into membership by avaricious leaders. They are entirely taken over by a power beyond their control. A provocative recent article argues,

> Literally, they are *possessed*, i.e., under the control of a separate personality or force that suppresses their own individual dispositions and uses them for purposes that they would normally not accept. Irrespective of the particular theory of demonology that may derive from a given theology, this phenomenology of attributed possession is not radically different from similar instances gleaned from the history of Christianity and other religions . . . . Other characteristics of the possessed, such as general physical debilitation, can be found in both historical and current cases.[194]

Since cult members are viewed as powerless to help themselves, their salvation must come from outside. Deprogramming thus comes to be presented as a type of exorcism; the deprogrammer expels the evil power which is controlling the cultist's mind, saves the individual from the baleful influence of the cult, and restores the individual's autonomy. As Proudfoot would have us suspect, the deprogrammer's description of the recent experience of the candidate for deprogramming contains as well an explanation of its origin. Patrick, as might be expected, does not explain his own activities as exorcism; he reads them in a rather different light. His intentions are mild and benign:

> I do not seek to implant in him any dogma, any pre-conceived or manufactured view or philosophy of life. Once he is deprogrammed he is absolutely free to do whatever he wants to do. Go to school, go to work, lie on a beach and look at the clouds. Whatever. That's none of my business. All I want and all I do is to return to them their ability to think for themselves, to exercise their free will, which the cults have put in cold storage. I thaw them out, and once they're free of the cult, with very

few exceptions they begin again to lead productive lives—and not necessarily conformist lives.[195]

My purpose here is not to embark on a thorough discussion of the nature and value of deprogramming, but rather to display its logic and to describe its affinity, on that level, with some other second order explanations of conversion. The image of the passive self, the self as the battleground of forces beyond its control,—be they psychological, sociological, historical, theological, or demonological—is a persistent feature in explanations of conversion advanced by both converts and outside observers. It articulates a basic interpretation of the process of conversion: something *happens to* the person in question.

What happens can be attributed to the Christian Holy Spirit (e.g. Stephen Bradley), Allah (e.g. Malcolm X), or evil cult leaders (e.g. Ted Patrick). It can also be attributed to and located in an observable process of social interaction. That is the approach most often taken by scholars from the social sciences who investigate the process of conversion to new religious movements. One of the best known and most influential examples of that explanatory option is a brief article by John Lofland and Rodney Stark, "Becoming a World-Saver."[196] Based primarily on extensive field research among the members of a fledgling messianic group on the West Coast, now known to be the early Unification Church, the article develops a model of the conversion process as it was described in the testimonies of some twenty early converts to the "Moonies."

The authors attempt to set their work in a broader context by observing that: "All men and all human groups have ultimate values, a world view, or a perspective furnishing them a more or less orderly and comprehensible picture of the world."[197] From that vantage point conversion can then be described as the process in which "a person gives up one such perspective or ordered view of the world for another."[198] The model Lofland and Stark propose consists of seven stages, not necessarily sequential, through which a person must pass in order to become fully converted to a "deviant perspective," like that of the Unification Church. The authors take account of both "predisposing conditions" and "situational contingencies" which influence the process of conversion. Briefly put, they argue that in order to become a full, as opposed to a "verbal," convert, a person must:

1. Experience enduring, acutely felt tensions
2. Within a religious problem-solving perspective,
3. Which leads him to define himself as a religious seeker;
4. Encountering the D.P. [Unification Church] at a turning point in his life,
5. Wherein an affective bond is formed (or pre-exists) with one or more converts;
6. Where extra-cult attachments are absent or neutralized;
7. And where, if he is to become a deployable agent, he is exposed to intensive interaction.[199]

The outlines of that model can be clarified through contrast. As James might state it, those who feel no persistent sense of uneasiness, or feel no profound division within themselves, are not likely candidates for conversion. Similarly, those who would incline to seek help for their perceived problems from another source, such as political action, psychological counseling, or immersion in drugs or alcohol, initially would not be prone to religious conversion. Also, those who feel that they have found satisfying religious certainty are less likely to change their views and affiliation. Moreover, one could encounter a conceivably attractive religious alternative at what is incontrovertibly the wrong time. Once introduced to a group, the potential convert might find its members, for whatever reasons, uninteresting or even personally repellent. In addition, affective ties with family, friends, and loved ones could well prove to be stronger than the pull of the new religious movement. Finally, one's interest might never move beyond a sort of passive dabbling, an interest but not a commitment. In brief, many things can happen, at any stage, that would short-circuit a conversion to a new religious movement like the Unification Church.[200] That helps to explain why the membership of such groups remains by all counts rather small.

Conversion to the Unification Church

In order to assess the usefulness of Lofland and

Stark's model of conversion it will be helpful to see it in action. Observers of the Unification Church are fortunate in that members of that group, like most converts, have been very willing to recount their conversion experiences. Nor have former members been reluctant to detail their own conversions into and out of the "Moonies." True believers and apostates alike urge on the reader their own explanations of their experience. In what follows, however, the focus will be shifted away from explanations offered by converts themselves to a second order explanation, using Lofland and Stark's model.

Born into a Roman Catholic family and a pious believer through his youth, Anthony experienced his first disillusionment with his church at age 12, when he began to read philosophy. He concluded at that point that "the Catholic nuns and priests that I knew were not a model for the life that I wanted to adopt."[201] Though he remained in the Roman Catholic educational system through college, Anthony retained at heart a certain skepticism. That attitude helped to coalesce for him a distinction between personal and institutional religion of which James would approve:

> It was my private reformation you might say,
> where I realized that you could separate your
> love for Jesus Christ from the Catholic church
> as an institution. And that was a profound
> experience, I do not want to belabor that
> because it didn't change my life in any way,
> and I didn't even think about it until several
> years later.[202]

In college his restless intellect turned to Marxism, but after studying it seriously for a year, he "concluded that it was irrational" and decided not to become a Marxist. His series of Augustinian encounters with books bearing wisdom continued:

> The following year I had a spiritual awakening
> and I shed my religious biases and became
> open spiritually again. This happened in a
> two-fold way: First, it was through the writ-
> ings of Soren Kierkegaard, who of course
> would appeal to me because of his attack on
> cultural Christianity. I realized that one could
> be against cultural Christianity and still find
> some essence, reality and meaningfulness in it.
> I actually had a profound conversion experi-
> ence to something (not God or Jesus). I

decided to totally change my life after reading Kierkegaard, and I went on a long fast that lasted over thirty days. I also gave the keys to my car away, trying to shed all of my material belongings. . . . I had what I might term a personal revelation.[203]

His revelation and his observation of the aftermath of the 1970 riots in Washington D.C, where he was living at the time, led Anthony to conclude that "we were living in the last days, that we were living in an apocalyptic, eschatological time."[204] The following year he met the "Moonies". After an initial encounter and conversation, one of the female Unification Church members visited him frequently over a period of a few months. Eventually he accepted her invitation to attend a weekend series of lectures on the *Divine Principle*, the central text of the Unificationist movement. He was strangely impressed: "This is a dirty trick. I thought I was just coming to some nice weekend, but if this is true, I'm going to have to change my entire lifestyle, and I wasn't prepared for that."[205] After reading on his own the *Divine Principle*, he reports,

> based on the testimonies that I heard from people after the workshop about their prayer life, I decided to begin praying seriously for the first time in my life. And in prayer I realized that God was a real being and that He was concerned for me. Finally, I had encountered the ground of my life, and in the relationship with God I found what I had been looking for.[206]

Those events took place during Anthony's junior year in college. He moved into the local Unification community at the end of the year. He offers this statement of the meaning of his conversion: "the Unification church and its teaching have helped me overcome my bias and resentment toward religion—actually toward God—and have opened up a tremendous relationship with God which I feel is the most essential thing in my life."[207]

Lofland and Stark's model helps to organize the process and clarify the structure of Anthony's conversion. Anthony's "problem-solving perspective" was certainly religious; even during his adolescent period of scepticism, religion, at least in its personal form, was never far away. His movement from the Catholicism of his youth to philosophical scepticism and then to Marxism and to Kierkegaard and finally to the

"Moonies" seems also to qualify him as a religious seeker in good standing. His conviction that he was "living in the last days" and his anxiety over the outcome of his spiritual experiences seem to indicate a certain enduring tension. Whether in the initial contact, at the weekend retreat, or in his private study, Anthony's encounter with the Unification Church marks a turning point in his life. The female Unificationist's frequent visits do seem to have established the rudiments of an affective bond, and Anthony gives no evidence of being strongly constrained by emotional ties to anyone outside the Church. His move into the local community and his subsequent career in the church, including his participation in the interfaith conference at which he gave his conversion testimony, show Anthony to be an active member and a "deployable agent." What Lofland and Stark's model does not illuminate is the depth and force of Anthony's final comment, but that belongs to a different realm of explanation.

Lofland and Stark's model highlights what *happened to* Anthony, particularly in the period from his initial encounter with the Unification Church to his joining their community. It operates on the premise of the passive self and aims to show how certain specific forms of social interaction led Anthony to exchange one "ordered view of the world" for another. There are several questions that might be posed concerning such an explanation. One of them concerns the extent to which conversion is adequately described and explained as a switch from one view of the world to another. Some conversion testimonies, and the explanations embedded in them, call that into question.

Patricia grew up in what she calls "a typical Catholic family."[208] Like Anthony's, all of her education, from grade school through college, was in parochial schools. Unlike Anthony, however, though she now sees herself as a Unificationist, she professes that she "did not have a religious conversion."[209] Patricia acknowledges that she had an avid interest in God and spiritual questions throughout her life. As she sees it, her intellectual and spiritual life constitutes a "search for truth."[210] Her restless quest disrupted her family life after college:

> Our family life became more problematic as I kept searching for more satisfactory spiritual experiences. . . . I began to feel that the more I sought spiritual answers the shakier our marriage became.[211]

An encounter with the Divine Light Mission[212] led Patricia to take drastic action, not unlike Anthony's after his collegiate personal religious experience:

> I quit my job, closed out my bank account, gave away my clothes. I was cooking food for hungry people, helping the poor as much as I could, trying to learn how to please God by being of service to others.[213]

Through her brother, who had earlier converted to the Unification Church, Patricia first met the teachings of the *Divine Principle*, to which she then devoted close attention amidst her other religious interests:

> I studied it pretty carefully for one month, while I kept going for meditation at my spiritual community of the Divine Light Mission. I was also praying and reading the Bible, and going to the Catholic Church on Sundays.[214]

On a trip to the Colorado ashram of the Divine Light Mission, Patricia also visited her brother at the Unification Church's Boulder center. She characterizes herself at that time as "twenty-eight years old and still searching for religious knowledge and spiritual peace."[215] At the Boulder center Patricia listened to the lectures about the Divine Principle and they changed her life:

> What happened there was that I really found God. Inside my heart God came to me as a real person, the God who created all things, who existed always, God the father, God the eternal, God the absolute. What I then realized was that God has a heart just like me, that he really has feelings just like me. I had a deep experience of discovery that really happened to me. Of course, God knew that I had been looking for him all my life. I had my ups and downs. I had lived in other countries. I had been lonely and often felt forsaken. Through the *Divine Principle* I now understood the Trinity. That was important for me to come to understand the source of all life. I understood God to be my father and my mother, that God was suffering, and that when I sin he suffers more.[216]

That account not only recalls Anthony's comment about developing "a tremendous relationship with God" but it also expresses several of the fundamental tenets of

Unification thought, especially the notion of God's "heart" or feelings, which can be affected by human activity such as sin. As James might observe, there is a congruence between Patricia's description of her experience and Unification theology.

Patricia's conversion led her to embrace the Unification Church, realizing that she has found in it her "permanent home."[217] But even though Patricia has joined a community of which she was not formerly a member, she does not believe that she has fundamentally changed her view of the world. Her own explanation is that "Moonies"

> continue to represent the Church we used to attend but with a different emphasis and more accurate destination. For example, I have looked for the good in the Catholic church, and I embrace it. I actually feel more strongly Catholic than I ever did in my life, and the reason is simple. I feel more the universality of Catholicism and what that really means when I say the Apostles' Creed. I feel that God is working everywhere through all religions, and I want to work together with people of all religions.[218]

Whether any Catholics, especially those in the hierarchy, would agree with Patricia's incorporation of Catholicism into the Unificationist ideology is beside the point. Her understanding of her conversion must first be dealt with on its own terms. As such, it raises a question about Lofland and Stark's basic characterization of conversion as a change in world-view. It is a question that Stark himself returned to in his later work.

In *The Future of Religion* Stark and his co-author William Sims Bainbridge express "dissatisfaction with any explanation that is limited to interrelating elements of meaning systems."[219] They insist that "meaning systems exist only as they have *social* meaning. All culture must be created, sustained, and transmitted."[220] Such a change in emphasis from the original Lofland and Stark model would allow them both to accept Patricia's description of her own experience and to maintain an explanation of it as conversion. Certainly, by Patricia's own admission, the social context of her continuing Catholicism has recognizably altered. Her social relations after entering the Unificationist movement have a different character and substance than they did before her conversion. She associates with different people and does different things. Even though Patricia believes that she thinks the same way, her thinking is taking place in a new and distinctively different context. Stark's later dissatisfaction with a narrow focus on world view as the locus of change allows him to sharpen the specifically sociological dimension of his analysis of conversion. That analysis both expresses and reinforces his general contention that "living religion is a social enterprise, and religious beliefs take on significance for human affairs only as they are tied to social exchanges."[221] That position also leads Stark to a firm rejection of the theological explanatory option favored by converts such as Stephen Bradley, Malcolm X, Augustine, and also by external observers such as by Barth and other theological interpreters of conversion. Stark and Bainbridge directly assert that "people do not join new religious movements on the basis of theological reflection, but only as they are linked to such movements by interpersonal bonds with group members."[222]

Stark's co-author of "Becoming a World-Saver" would probably agree. But Lofland, too, would now revise some of the emphases of that first attempt to explain the process of conversion in sociological terms. In an article aptly entitled "Becoming a World-Saver Revisited" Lofland concedes that the early efforts at conversion that he and Stark observed among the "Moonies" "were in many respects weak, haphazard, and bumbling."[223] Beginning in the early seventies, however, the Unification Church developed "one of the most ingenious, sophisticated, and effective conversion organizations ever devised."[224] Lofland describes how the new missionary tactics enabled the Unificationists to overcome a persistent dilemma: the more they disclosed their distinctive beliefs at the outset, the less potential converts were likely to join. Lofland divides the new recruiting process into "five, quasi-temporal phases: picking-up, hooking, encapsulating, loving, and committing."[225] More so than in his previous model, Lofland now depicts the new religious movement as actively pursuing and cultivating potential converts in a much more purposive manner. Christopher Edwards gives a riveting account of the success of that change in missionary strategy in the intense and painful story of his brief career as a "Moonie," Crazy for God.

Christopher graduated from Yale in 1975. Like Anthony and Patricia, he was a seeker. He had for some time "hoped to discover the meaning of my life with all its confusions."[226] Tension built as he was unable to find the meaning he sought; he counted his time in college as "four years of increasing disillusionment as I saw my utopian dreams and intellectual castles come tumbling down . . ."[227] At the end of his final year, Christopher had an experience that turned him to religion:

> But one spring night sitting in my room, writing a senior paper on developmental psychology, my body was gripped by waves of fear as I suddenly realized that perhaps the true, the ultimate answers to life I was seeking must come from beyond the intellect. Perhaps *knowledge was not to be discovered but received.* I considered the words of Jesus: "Ask and it shall be given to you; seek and ye shall find." And so with everything to gain and nothing to lose, I fell to my knees and begged:

> "Lord, if ever there is, if ever there was, a Creator, if there exists a being great enough to love me, to answer my questions, to give me my life—O God, O God, if you are out there and if you care, touch me—touch me please!"

> Suddenly, just as suddenly as they had begun, the waves disappeared and I found myself at peace. Astonished, I asked: "O Lord, are you really there, or is this some sort of supreme joke?"

> The crown of my head began to tingle. Streams of love—for lack of a better word— began flowing through my body like a mysterious current of bliss. I was overcome by joy.[228]

After that, Christopher began to read the Bible, "determined to search, to go anywhere to achieve such transcendence."[229] At the same time his close relationship with a woman had dissolved; in his words: "I had turned inward and she had turned to an Iraqi Marxist."[230] In that state of mind Christopher graduated and left for California.

Almost as soon as he set foot in Berkeley, Christopher was invited to dinner by a friendly stranger. Jacob told Christopher that he was involved with a "loving, very idealistic group of young people" that conducted a number of community projects in the area. After some initial hesitance and a suspicious query about the religious nature of the group, Christopher accepted the invitation. He was picked up. At dinner that evening Christopher was virtually beseiged by friendly young people. They welcomed him effusively; complimented his clothing; inquired solicitously about his well being, background, and interests; and engaged him in conversation about his goals and values. They were very kind and very attentive:

> After asking me a personal question, Family members would respond to my answer by saying how much their situation was like mine. They seemed to be playing upon my identity, deliberately trying to draw me close. I resented this intrusion on a life that was uniquely mine, but I felt more bewildered than resentful. Just what were they up to?[231]

Entertainment and a lecture followed dinner, as did an invitation from Christopher's new friends to spend a weekend with them at a farm in the country. Christopher agreed; he had been hooked. At the farm, he was plunged into a strenuous regimen of organized activities, including exercise, singing, group discussions, and more lectures. Any questions about the meaning and intent of all those activities were put off until later. Participation, not explanation, was stressed: " 'Just keep singing, Chris,' Mitch encouraged me. 'Later you'll understand.' "[232] Another weekender chastened Christopher: "Now don't be negative, Chris! Try to smile and have a good time. You'll understand everything after you hear the lectures."[233] The lectures come and go, leaving Christopher with even more questions. But as he moves through the weekend's routine, enveloped by the ever-present concern of the members of long standing, Christopher is constantly being urged, persuaded, or even coerced *to act like* a member of the group, whatever his intellectual disposition:

> "Whatsamatter, Chris? We can't hear you. Chant louder," Jackie shouted. I complied.
>
> "C'mon, you can chant louder than that." I chanted still louder. It suddenly flashed through my mind that I was beginning to automatically comply with any order I was given, but the thought was gone before it had really registered. The game soon ended, and we filed back to the Chicken Palace for our last lecture of the day.[234]

As aware as he is of what is happening, Christopher is not immune to its attraction. During communal singing, he recalls: "Ecstatically, I merged into the mass, tasting the glorious pleasure that accompanies the loss of the ego. How desperately I sought unity among all people."[235] In a setting perfectly designed to accomplish it, Christopher has become encapsulated into the world of his new friends. He has entered their life and felt their love. Their constant attention has rendered his participation and his eventual commitment plausible by frequently providing evidence of social support. As Berger and Luckman might put it, the religious community of Unificationists at the ranch consistently encourages Christopher to keep on taking his experience as a fledgling member seriously.

Observers as diverse as Ted Patrick and Wayne Proudfoot have commented on the role of such social pressure in eliciting and securing conversion. In Patrick's characteristically blunt formulation: "They don't let a kid sleep, they don't let him eat. They hit him with tape recordings of Scripture, lectures, discussions, workshops—night and day. They wear him down, wear him out. Pretty soon he believes anything."[236] As a more disinterested analyst, Proudfoot too acknowledges that:

> Many religious communities urge prospective
> converts to engage in ritual action or discipline
> before they acquaint themselves with the sup-
> porting doctrine. . . . Each of these activities
> engages a person. Once involved in the action,
> he is more susceptible to adopting the beliefs of
> the community in order to justify his actions
> and explain his feelings.[237]

Both Patrick and Proudfoot point precisely to those aspects of the conversion process that sociologists like Lofland and Stark deem to be of paramount importance. Commitment and belief travel through a web of social relations. Such relations can be firmly established before any full intellectual acceptance of doctrine; in fact, the development of affective bonds will hasten intellectual assent.

As Chrisopher's initial weekend at the farm stretched into a week, he was drawn deeper into the group. Their affection for him was evident: "Listening to Chris, I became inspired that the Truth can appeal to different people in so many different ways. Chris is so intelligent and so well prepared to hear the Truth."[238] He meets their encapsulating love at every turn:

> Chris, I've been praying a whole lot for you.
> And I want you to know that Heavenly Father
> wants you here so very much. He loves you
> and misses you, has missed you for six thou-

sand years, ever since we fell from God. I wish we had more brothers and sisters like you. I feel very close to you.[239]

When Christopher finally learns that his new comrades accept the Reverend Moon as their teacher, he resolves to "escape" from the farm. He oversleeps, however, and is drawn back into the communal routine. Simultaneously attracted and repelled by his experience at the farm, Christopher wrestles with a classically divided self: "I sat back to think, struggling as Old Life feelings and New Life feelings battled within me."[240] At the end of his first full week Christopher takes stock:

> At first I viewed the Heavenly Kingdom as a possibility to be tested, but as the week progressed I began to accept it much more literally. I embraced what I wanted to believe so badly, the chance to live for something I could die for, to live and die for a love eternal, a love so strong that by its own whim it could command life or death.[241]

Finally, the overwhelming experience of his new friends' acceptance of him breaks down Christopher's resistance: "Nobody had ever loved me so much, nobody had really cared. . . . This was where I wanted to stay, where I could be loved and accepted. This was the place where God wanted me to be . . ."[242] Christopher, in his heart, commits to the Unification Church.

As Lofland and Stark's original article suggests, it is but a short step from commitment to becoming a "deployable agent" or an active proselytizer. Proudfoot also notes that engaging in proselytizing is a particularly effective way of creating and reinforcing commitment.[243] In fact, very soon after committing to the group, Christopher was instructing newcomers about the proper behavior of aspiring "Heavenly Children" in the Family, describing his own progress in conversion during group discussions, pouring out his love on likely new recruits, and generally manifesting his zeal for the coming kingdom. The words of an old hand proved to be eerily prophetic: "Just trust us. We'll remake you into a new person, a real heavenly child. Just you wait."[244] After a month Christopher left the farm to return to Berkeley, a total convert to the Unification Church.

Lofland's characterization of the new, improved conversion tactics of the Unification Church is thoroughly confirmed by Christopher's admittedly hostile account. Though it depicts the "Moonies" themselves as much more active and organized in their search for converts, it still relies on the powerful image of the passive self. Christopher is picked up, hooked, encapsulated, and loved. His social circumstances and his personal relationships are manipulated in such a way as to produce his commitment. His conversion *happens to him*. Though to some extent that view expresses the distinctive perspective of sociological analysis, Lofland himself identifies a missing dimension.

At the close of "Becoming a World-Saver Revisited" Lofland writes that he has "come to appreciate that the world-saver model embodies a thoroughly "passive" actor—a conception of humans as a 'neutral medium through which social forces operate.' "[245] He argues that it may be time "to turn the process on its head and to scrutinize how people go about converting themselves."[246] The image of the passive self need not be a necessary feature of either primary or secondary explanations of conversion. That image, even when it is embedded by converts in descriptions of their own experience, is actually part of an explanation. Even when it is taken over by theologians like Rahner and Barth or sociologists like Lofland and Stark, it remains part of an explanation and therefore not a necessary element of the described experience. Explanations, whether first order or second order, reflect and express the interests and convictions of those doing the explaining. To use the image of the passive self in the explanation of the process of conversion is to make an (often implicit) interpretive decision. Other decisions are, of course, possible.

Again, the issue can be made more vivid and comprehensible by moving from the theoretical level to the level of described experience. Barbara Underwood's account of her movement into and out of the Unification Church in *Hostage to Heaven* furnishes an example of a primary explanation of conversion that does not rely totally on the image of the passive self. In its broad outlines Barbara's story does not differ radically from those of Anthony, Patricia, and Christopher considered earlier in this chapter. Barbara initially intended to conduct participant-observer research on the Unification Church for a sociology project at the University of California at Santa Cruz. A friend from school, however, had already joined the Oakland "Family," and Barbara remained quite aware of that option:

> I remember my first introduction to the Family. I went on impulse to visit Joanna, who'd

left Santa Cruz to join a mysterious communal
setup in Oakland where there was a lot of talk
in old-fashioned terms about love and duty to
the collective goals. In that old house on Dana
Street in Oakland and on their Boonville farm
[the same farm where Christopher had stayed],
I found a group of people, mostly my age,
living in such a close way I couldn't believe it.
When I heard all their old-fashioned rules of
moral conduct, I thought *what absurdities* and
then I went away. But afterward, I couldn't
think of anything else except that weekend and
those good, solid, happy faces. I decided I
would have to move in sometime in the future,
at least for a short time, and then finish up at
Santa Cruz. But somewhere brewed intimations
of a long-term commitment.[247]

Although Barbara remains aware throughout her narrative of the "overwhelmingly seductive power" of experience within the controlled confines of the group, she
consistently portrays herself as an active author of her
fate. At the outset of her association with the group, she
declares to her mother: "I want to test the ability of the
individual person to change, then change society."[248]
Through entries in a journal that she kept during her life
as a "Moonie", Barbara reveals herself to be constantly
sifting through what she heard and searching for its
truth.[249] She acknowledges the powerful constraining
force of her new social circumstances and relationships[250] but strives to retain a sense of self[251] and to
examine critically her new life.[252] Even on the verge of a
court hearing to consider her parents' request for a
temporary conservatorship over her, Barbara remembers
possessing a steady self-centered resolve: "I was determined to be faithful to the past four years of my life, to
those years devoted unconditionally to loving and serv-
ing God, which is all I really cared about and all I still
really care about."[253] Barbara's testimony includes the
expected recognition of the power of social pressure, but
it is also noteworthy for its refusal to collapse that
awareness into a central image of the passive self, acted
upon and not acting. As she waits for the judge's
decision, Barbara expresses her own ambivalence: "As a
follower of Sun Myung Moon, I was afraid for the
conservatorship to be granted. As myself, I was afraid
for it *not* to be granted, because by now something
buried deep in me was screaming for the truth, whatever
it might be."[254] When the conservatorship is granted to

her parents, Barbara finds it difficult to describe herself as a passive victim:

> I couldn't make myself give a statement to the
> press about my civil rights being snatched away
> as I moved through the uproarious halls.
> Outraged as I was, somehow I also felt I was
> shedding a captive skin.
>
> As I climbed into the deprogrammer's car, I
> was determined to find God alone in my walk
> through the wilderness to come.[255]

During the period of her "deprogramming," in fact, Barbara carefully negotiates her way between the pressures exerted by family and friends to leave the group and the urgent demands by some of those in the community she had left that she stand up to those pressures and re-affirm her membership.

In Ted Patrick's formulation, the process of deprogramming returns to its subjects the free will of which they had been deprived by the devious tricks of unscrupulous cult leaders:

> All I want and all I do is to return to them
> their ability to think for themselves, to exercise
> their free will, which the cults have put into
> cold storage. I thaw them out, and once
> they're free of the cult, with very few excep-
> tions they begin again to lead productive
> lives—and not necessarily conformist lives.[256]

That drama of the reawakening of the passive self finds little confirmation in Barbara's account of her own deprogramming. From the beginning she takes responsibility for whatever transformation has occurred. Remembering her state of mind as the trial began, she writes:

> Later I would know that if anything could have
> deprogrammed me it would be the process,
> begun at the hearing, of realizing contradictions
> in my own ability to act within the Church in a
> truthful way. *My growing consciousness of my
> own lost integrity was what ultimately
> deprogrammed me.*[257]

Barbara rejects an explanation of her own conversion into and out of the "Moonies" that depends upon an image of the passive self. While she admits the strong influence of social circumstances and personal relationships on her joining the movement and on her leaving it, Barbara portrays both events as her own decisions:

> I joined the Unification Church because I thought I'd found the ultimate truth. I left the cult because I realized during the course of the courtroom hearing and of my deprogramming —in an environment where I was free for the first time in four years to reflect, question, and examine—that the truth wasn't black and white. I discovered it wasn't that my own faith in God was inauthentic; I'd wrongly worshipped a "God" that Moon's Principles had created in my mind, a "God" who mistrusted individual freedom of will.[258]

Barbara's comments blend a frank appreciation of the Unificationists' attempts to influence her with an insistence that she knew what she was doing all along. She does not recall having been hypnotized, kidnapped, or brainwashed. She was "programmed" in the ways that all human beings are programmed: through their participation in social life. One of the interesting consequences of Barbara's rejection of an explanation of her conversions that depends upon the image of the passive self is that she rejects as well any demonization of the group to which she had belonged. The "Moonies" remain for her real people, with all the attendant flaws and virtues, not superhuman demonic adversaries. She remembers with evident affection her friends in the group and still cherishes many of the ideals that led her to join. Barbara introduces a welcome note of complexity to the discussion of conversion into and out of new religious movements:

> Within the Church or without, there are no ultimate victors and no easily defined enemies. And within the Unification membership there are decent but fallible human beings demonstrating a desire to love, to weave myth, to claim for themselves the glory of God. Unfortunately, the passion for God and goodness can lead to severe violations of the freedom of the individual. And worse. . . .
>
> Having seen both sides of the issues involved, I have no easy answers.[259]

As I have argued before, whatever answers are proposed will express a particular explanation. Such explanations, whether they come from the subjects themselves or from external observers, indicate and depend upon general theoretical understandings of religion. Primary explanations almost always imply partial and fragmented theories of religion. Neither Stephen Bradley, Malcolm X, nor Christopher Edwards is a particularly impressive theorist on that count. Secondary explanations typically have more direct links to general theories. Lofland and Stark's original "Becoming a World-Saver," for example, essentially equated religion with world-view.[260] Stark, however, later expressed dissatisfaction with such a formulation since it did not direct sufficient attention to the social location of systems of meaning, a self-evidently important concern for sociologists.[261] In his most recent work Stark has attempted to set his discussion of conversion within the framework of an explicit sociological theory of religion. It is, of course, not the only such theory, but it provides an adequate example of that explanatory approach.

A Sociological Theory of Religion

In *The Future of Religion* Stark and Bainbridge identify the basic problem in defining religion as attaining the appropriate level of generality. On the one hand, the definition should apply equally well to systems commonly recognized as religious, such as the various forms of Christianity and Buddhism, the religion of the Dogon of Mali, and the traditional religion of Bali. On the other, they argue, it should not apply equally well to complexes of belief and practice that are in some ways similar to but remain distinct from religion, such as Marxism, or the American Association of Atheists. The authors take as their key defining characteristic a belief in supernatural beings.[262] They claim that a definition of religion as necessarily involving belief in supernatural beings will enable them to identify as religious most, if not all, forms of Buddhism, for example, and to identify as not religious, despite various functional similarities, ideologies such as Marxism which profess no such belief. Whatever the adequacy of such a definition,[263] its impact on the description and explanation of conversion is obvious. Religious conversion will have to involve in some fashion belief in supernatural beings. Anthony's sceptical disengagement from the institutional Catholic church would accordingly be viewed as a conversion out of religion, as would Christopher's and Barbara's departure from the Unification Church. Whether Christopher and Barbara left the "Moonies" for another religious group would depend on their supernatural beliefs; her participation in deprogramming activities, in itself, could not be construed as a religious conversion.

Stark and Bainbridge argue further that religions are "human organizations primarily engaged in providing general compensators based on supernatural assumptions."[264] The mention of organizations signals their basic contention that religion is primarily a social, not an individual affair.[265] They define a compensator as "the belief that a reward will be obtained in the distant future or in some other context which cannot be immediately verified."[266] That focus on rewards depends on the general axiom that "humans seek what they perceive to be rewards and try to avoid what they perceive to be costs."[267] Further, the stress on general compensators allows them to distinguish between religion and magic, since the latter offers only limited, specific compensators.[268] The technical discussion eventually depends on a simple observation: "Some common human desires are so beyond direct, this-worldly satisfaction that only the gods can provide them."[269] Stark and Bainbridge remain aware, however, that religions offer more to their adherents than deferred gratification through general compensating beliefs. To take account of the direct tangible rewards obtainable in religion through human action and interaction, they discuss religious commitment in three dimensions. The worldly dimension is the realm of relatively immediate, concrete rewards, including earning a living, the exercise of power, and the acquisition of prestige. The other-worldly dimension concerns the ways that religions "can assuage worldly suffering by emphasizing the better life to come."[270] Finally, the universal dimension is where those universal human concerns, common to everyone alike, find their response; it is the proper location for answers to questions about the meaning of life or the nature and destiny of the universe. In all of their analysis, Stark and Bainbridge claim, "It is not our intent to suggest anything about the truth of religion. We seek only to discover its visible aspects—the social forms it takes in the world we all can see."[271] Consequently, they do not discuss precisely that element, the theological, which is crucial to primary explanations of virtually all converts and to some types of secondary explanation as well.

Even on its own terms, however, Stark and Bainbridge's theory of religion skirts some of the same problems that cropped up in the Lofland and Stark article on "Becoming a World-Saver" some twenty years earlier. The discussion of compensators and dimensions revolves to a great extent around questions of belief and meaning. The nature and importance of religions as "human organizations" is virtually taken for granted, though they do attempt to define the various types of organization, including churches, sects, and cults. When the discussion turns to conversion, however, the fundamentally social nature of religion occupies center stage. Stark and Bainbridge assert that even "if most of the needs served by religion are individual, the sources of faith are social."[272] It is extraordinarily difficult for individuals to invent their own religious beliefs and then maintain that belief without social support. People gain faith, Stark and Bainbridge argue, from social relationships, not primarily from their individual thoughts and circumstances. They would contend, in contrast to James, that the "feelings, acts, and experiences of individual men in their solitude" can only become and remain religion in some sort of social context. As Berger and Luckmann state in the remark quoted at the beginning of this chapter: "To have a conversion experience is nothing much. The real thing is to be able to keep on taking it seriously; to retain a sense of its plausibility. *This* is where the religious community comes in."[273]

Conclusions

The contention that people do not join new religious movements for theological reasons but because they form interpersonal bonds with group members sets for Stark and Bainbridge an agenda for the study of conversion. It directs attention to processes like the ones that Lofland identified in "Becoming a World-Saver Revisited." As Christopher Edwards' narrative in *Crazy for God* indicates, analysis of his social interaction with various members of the Unification Church through the stages identified by Lofland does much to clarify the process and substance of his conversion. The perspective of sociologists also significantly illuminates the conversions of Anthony, Patricia, and Barbara, and it could plausibly be extended to the cases of Malcolm X, Augustine of Hippo, and Stephen Bradley, where sufficient information is available. But as Lofland's later comments and the testimony of Barbara Underwood suggest, the generic sociological explanation of conversion, in surprising tandem with the generic theological explanation, depends to a great extent on the image of the passive self. While that may well represent an interpretive choice that many observers are quite willing to make, there does seem to be room, even within the generic sociological explanation, for a fuller investigation of what Lofland calls the ways in which "people go about converting themselves." In the following chapter I will discuss another case which lends credence to that suspicion. In some respects it does seem to make sense to focus on individuals as the agents of their own conversions. That is not to deny, however, that individuals are, as the sociologists considered in this chapter would agree, often caught up in relationships and processes that are not wholly within their control. The second part of the next chapter will focus on how the decisions that individuals make in conversion are implicated in broader social and historical currents.

Chapter 4

Conversion in Africa: The Autonomous Self and Cultural History

Lofland's theoretical suggestion, coupled with Barbara Underwood's description of her own conversion, indicates that it is possible, and even desirable, to include in explanations of conversion some appreciation of the active role that people play in bringing about their own self-transformations. In some instances that may mean explicitly rejecting, in part or whole, the individual's primary explanation of conversion. Augustine, for example, insists that he was not able to bring about his conversion to Catholic Christianity. Nevertheless, from a perspective outside of his experience, it is clear that his restless intellectual searching certainly contributed to his conversion. Much the same could be said for the cases considered in the previous chapter; Anthony, Patricia, Christopher, and Barbara identified themselves in one way or another as religious seekers. Malcolm X did not see himself as a religious seeker before his conversion to the Nation of Islam, but he does acknowledge his active role in sifting through their teachings and comparing them to his own experience. Those cases suggest that in developing an adequate explanation of conversion it may be possible to blend both a recognition of the powerful influence of external forces (be they imminent or transcendant) with an acknowledgment of the individual's active role in perceiving and reacting to such forces. Such an explanation would have to be based both on a convert's account and on an observer's appraisal of the external forces involved.

An African Conversion

One of the most striking accounts of an individual's conversion in recent literature occurs in Bennetta Jules-Rosette's *African Apostles: Ritual and Conversion in the Church of John Maranke*. As a doctoral candidate at Harvard, Jules-Rosette decided to conduct research on African Independent Christian Churches.[274] She travelled to Zaire to study the Apostolic Church of John Maranke, an organization founded in 1932 which could claim over 150,000 adherents in several African countries by the early 1970s. During the course of her field work Jules-Rosette herself converted to the church; she turned from being an anthropological participant-observer to an "observing participant." As a social scientist who became a convert to the group she studied, Jules-Rosette is well positioned to report on the self in transformation within its social context.

Like the various converts in the previous chapter, Jules-Rosette is well aware of the social pressures exerted upon her. From her initial encounter, she suspects that the Bapostolo (the "Apostles" of John Maranke) consider her a potential convert. The church members welcomed her, "certain that I would inspire many baptisms in the United States."[275] They subsequently interpreted her willingness to travel to an annual Passover ceremony as an indication of her readiness to be baptized into the church.[276] When Jules-Rosette questioned members about their conversions, some of them turned the occasion into an opportunity to encourage her own conversion. From the beginning of her stay with them, the members of John Maranke's church remained absolutely certain that their visitor from the United States (and her husband, who plays a largely silent but intriguing role in her account) would become a member.

The Bapostolo missionary efforts were not as elaborate and sophisticated as those of the Unification Church. They simply took every opportunity to encourage Jules-Rosette's conversion, whether in direct conversation or by indirect control of her situation. The Apostles' interaction with Jules-Rosette seems less to reflect a carefully thought-out recruiting strategy—such as the hooking, picking up, encapsulating, loving, and commitment described by Lofland—and more a direct expression of their faith that Jules-Rosette's arrival had an immediate religious meaning. The Apostles simply urged Jules-Rosette to demonstrate the truth of their convictions by accepting baptism. Her journey from being an anthropological observer to an "observing participant" in the life of the Apostolic Church is a gradual one, but it reaches a climax when she is invited to attend the Apostles' major yearly ritual at a site some distance away from her temporary residence in Zaire. When Jules-Rosette arrives at the site of the annual Passover celebration, her understanding of her role within the community and the Apostles' understanding of that role come into explicit conflict. Since only Apostles can participate in the Passover ceremony, she is told that on the next day she would either have to declare herself a candidate for baptism or leave the compound.[277]

Jules-Rosette did not leave, and she became a member of the Bapostolo through baptism the next day. Her baptism was punctuated by a distinctive visionary experience which recalls in some ways the experience of Stephen Bradley or Augustine. Such visions are expected to be part of the experience of entering the Church of John Maranke; the founder himself had experienced many such visions, which revealed and confirmed his status as a messenger of God before his own baptism.[278] Jules-Rosette's vision brings together many elements of her prior experience with the Apostolic Chruch. While waiting in a hut for the ceremony to begin, Jules-Rosette

> watched the wall, [and] a radiant six-pointed
> star appeared. It seemed filled in on two
> corners with red patches and on the others
> with white, blue, and yellow patches. The
> outline of the star was a shiny copper. Momen-
> tarily, this star, about five feet in width, was
> vividly present, flashing three times like a neon
> sign. Then it disappeared.[279]

Neither Jules-Rosette nor any one else offers an explanation of that inital experience. Next, as she emerged from the baptismal pool, Jules-Rosette "again saw the copper star."[280] Finally:

> After returning to the hut, I glimpsed the star
> once more, with strange, illegible letters under
> it. An encompassing voice that was not loud
> yet seemed to fill all of the space said: "Go to
> the Jews," three times. . . . Once the star faded
> away, three bottles of medicine stood before me
> as if glued to the wall. One was large and
> black, with a white skull and cross-bones

emblazoned on the front. Another was red, smaller, also with a skull and crossbones. The smallest bottle was white, without the skull and crossbones. A voice said that I was not to touch the first two bottles that contained manmade medicines, but only the third, very small clear bottle filled with oil and water.[281]

The third vision contains elements of its own explanation. It clearly relates to the Apostles' long-standing expectation that Jules-Rosette would become a successful missionary for the church in the United States. Later, one of the Apostles confirmed that understanding of the vision by linking it to Jesus' charge to the disciples in Matthew 10:5 to preach to "the lost sheep of Israel." The second part of the third vision also relates to Jules-Rosette's previous experience with the group. Shortly before leaving for the Passover service in Malawi, Jules-Rosette had become very sick. As she recalls:

> None of my patent medicines seemed to help. When the evangelist Tshiaba saw my condition, he volunteered to pray for me. . . . Dressed in a blue robe, Tshiaba placed the Bible over a tin cup of water. He prayed slowly and quietly, then handed me the cup. I became nauseous and was unable to keep even the water on my stomach, but my entire body felt cleansed. A few hours later, I was able to drink tea with some other members, while they sang and prayed. This was my first experience of purposive sharing in the reality of ceremony.[282]

The baptismal vision of the bottles thus suggests a confirmation of the Apostles' acceptance of spiritual healing and rejection of Western medicine. Jules-Rosette's vision is thus connected with her previous experience in a network of relationships with members of the Apostolic community. As she testifies, the substance of that experience, including the Apostles' fond hopes for her imminent conversion and career as a missionary and her initial healing, prepared her to accept both baptism and the attendant visions as meaningful events. The instruction that she received after her baptism, and her increased participation in Apostolic life, enabled Jules-Rosette to solidify and extend the meaning of her act of conversion.

Through the social relationships that they formed with Jules-Rosette, the Bapostolo exerted an even and continuous pressure for her conversion. After her baptism they provided the supportive context in which she could come to a progressively deeper understanding of its significance. Before her baptism, being true to her professional commitment, Jules-Rosette was immersing herself in Apostolic way of life. Simply living with the group as a participant-observer creates a change in her own life:

> . . . I had learned and consciously reflected on the Apostolic way of life by living among members. I was already learning Apostolic songs, following dietary laws, and associating largely with members of the Apostolic community in each town that I visited. But before the Malawi trip [to the Passover celebration] the obligations of membership were not binding upon me, and I could shift out of the frame of reference of the Apostolic community without confession, guilt, or direct spiritual scrutiny.[283]

Living *with* the Bapostolo is separated from living *as* a member of the group by the act of personal commitment. Jules-Rosette sees the difference as she pursues her academic agenda; at first, in conversation with the Bapostolo: "It seemed impossible that I would ever understand the reasoning behind their questions or the assumptions that they were making about me."[284] As an outsider, Jules-Rosette finds herself barred not only from certain ritual practices but also from a coherent explanation of the puzzling variety of Bapostolo beliefs and practices. She eventually argues that it was only through accepting membership that she could arrive at an adequate explanation of Apostolic beliefs and practices:

> Insofar as my aims were to uncover how members think and feel about the world, these experiences were the primary data that would have been unavailable without my membership. Another account could only have returned for its auspices to the points of reference of the reporter.[285]

That comment represents a radical extension of Proudfoot's contention that an adequate description of another's experience must be one that can plausibly be attributed to the subject.[286] Whether membership is *necessary* to the process of description should at least remain open to discussion; that it afforded Jules-Rosette a special vantage point is beyond question.

Becoming a member of the Church of John Maranke immeasurably increased Jules-Rosette's understanding of their religion. Her conversion enabled her to participate in rituals she previously knew only second-hand; after conversion she was immersed in an extended period of instruction, both formal and informal. She continued to learn about the Apostolic way of life by living it, but it now became normative and authoritative for her. In her own words:

> The explanations of specific forms of behavior for a particular occasion intensified after I joined the group, although they continued to seem arbitrary. I was told how to dress, where and how to sit, when to wash, and how to eat. No aspect of my life was outside of the scrutiny of male or female elders. No action went without comment, ridicule, or occasionally, a smile of approval at some minimal mastery. Many of the notes I took early in my membership re-emphasized what I then felt to be constant criticism but what I now see in retrospect as terse but well-meant instruction. Part of the dramatic impact of the conversion experience emerged through examining it and constructing it in retrospect.[287]

Even as Jules-Rosette struggles to comprehend the implications of her baptism, she does so within the context of the Apostolic community and its specific beliefs and practices. Along with her fellow Apostles, she begins to think out and live out the implications of her conversion; every subsequent action, every social encounter, can add depth and nuance to her understanding of that experience. Jules-Rosette would likely agree with Berger and Luckmann's statement, quoted in the previous chapter, that it is much less difficult to have an experience of conversion than it is to maintain it. She correctly observes that "acceptance is neither permanent nor ensured by baptism, an outward symbol of conversion, for it must be constantly reinforced by fresh evaluations of emerging situations."[288] For rather different reasons, she might be tempted to agree with Barth's characterization of conversion as a way of life rather than a momentary experience.

Jules-Rosette's attempts to comprehend the Apostolic way of life and the Apostles' desire for her conversion meet at the moment of her baptism. What she wants and what they want fuse in what she becomes. As a fledgling Apostle, Jules-Rosette begins to see and understand the world in a new way. She argues that in general "the conversion experience restructures basic expectations about the representations of a previously

known reality."[289] Fundamental categories of thought
are re-formed:

> These spiritual reinterpretations of reality
> include changes in conceptions of time, space,
> and social relationships. Ceremonial time
> becomes the time that it takes to experience a
> performance, including absorption in chants
> through which Apostles assert that they obtain
> a glimpse of Heaven, bypassing the standard
> time and reality orientations of mundane inter-
> action. The place of prayer, similarly, comes to
> be seen as a new Jerusalem, a protected Heaven
> on earth endowed with this timeless quality.
> Social relationships are transformed in this
> spirit world in which a unity of purpose attunes
> members to a new order of existence.[290]

A new way of thinking and a new way of living
reinforce each other; the crucial difference in Jules-
Rosette's post-baptismal life is that the obligations of
membership now are binding on her. Membership
becomes her way of life, something that she *does*, not an
external phenomenon, something she *observes*.

Despite her evident appreciation of the influence of
social context, Jules-Rosette's understanding of her own
conversion is not predicated upon an image of the
passive self. Apostolic doctrine about conversion and her
own thinking about her personal transformation both
depend upon an image of the active, decision-making
self. For the Apostles, "acceptance was always a
voluntary act."[291] As one member put it in a sermon,
"Who wants to join us will do so deliberately, so does
whoever wants to quit. We do not have any strings
attached to our faith."[292] As Jules-Rosette recalls,
"Deliberate acceptance in my case consisted of *a
commitment* to new possibilities and guidelines for life
without knowing specifically what these might entail."[293]
Despite the uncertain character of the future, Jules-
Rosette resolved to forge ahead; she "had consciously
chosen the baptism"[294] and thereafter strived to fulfill
the Apostles' expectations of her.

If Barbara Underwood might sum up her experience
with the Moonies by claiming: "I got myself into this
and I got myself out of it," so would Jules-Rosette
describe her conversion as a conscious act undertaken
within specific social circumstances. In both cases, the
testimony introduces an alternative explanatory element,
the image of the active self. Jules-Rosette's account

differs from Underwood's only in its relatively greater sophistication in reporting the effects of the social and cultural matrix.

Explanations of conversion that feature an image of the active self might also help to account for the abundant diversity in conversion narratives. The four "Moonies" and ex-"Moonies" of the previous chapter seem both to have had rather different experiences and to explain them in different ways. Neither a facile generalization about the superhuman hypnotic powers of cult members nor airy pieties about God's loving heart are sufficient to explain that diversity. It seems more useful to acknowledge the role that individuals themselves play in sifting through what they hear about and experience in the group in question. Such an explanatory approach is an implicit part of Jules-Rosette's description and explanation of her own conversion. Of course, her dual role of ethnographer and convert heightens and complicates her awareness of the questions she asks and the decisions she makes.[295]

An explanation founded on the image of the active self could potentially make sense, for example, both of Patricia's continuing respect for her Catholicism and of Barbara Underwood's movement into and out of the Unification Church. It could enable the observer to identify both patterns of similarity and the distinctive differences of conversion accounts even within a single religious tradition. Proudfoot argues that "the often rather subtle doctrinal differences between religious communities, or subgroups of the same community, will give rise to different experiences."[296] Without denying the tendency for an "admirable congruity" to develop between the ideology of a particular group and the accounts of converts into that group, it may be possible to identify as well, where there is sufficient evidence, the distinctively individual contributions to the process of conversion. An image of the active, as opposed to the passive, self could be the key to such an approach.

My discussion of explanations that depend on images of the passive or active self differs from James' distinction between volitional conversion and conversion by self-surrender in one important way. Where James' stated goal was to characterize the *experience* of conversion, I want to redirect the focus to the *explanation* of conversion. In my terms, the converts considered by James *have chosen*, implicitly or explicitly, to portray and explain their experience in certain ways. Those who favor the image of the active self are more likely to describe their conversion as volitional. In contrast, those who, because of personal, psychological, or theological commitments, favor an image of the passive self will tend to describe their conversions as self-surrender. The same would hold true on the level of secondary explanations. The shift in focus that I propose depends upon the recognition that converts' stories contain both descriptive and explanatory elements.

Explanations using an image of the active self portray conversion as something that people *do* within certain religious, social, and cultural contexts. In the cases considered so far, however, the context has been primarily *local*. Both in Jules-Rosette's account and in the instances of conversion discussed in the previous chapters, converts have typically situated themselves in a web of relationships that did not extend much further than their family, friends, and acquaintances. Lofland and Stark's initial model, for example, concentrated on the relatively narrow horizons of the individual convert. It described the immediate predisposing conditions and situational contigencies that could lead an individual to convert to a group espousing a "deviant perspective." Jules-Rosette similarly focuses on the contribution to her conversion of her own local interactions with various members of John Maranke's church. Only Malcolm X attempted to set his own experience, and that of black people in general, within a broad historical context. In fact, the ability of the doctrine of the Nation of Islam to make sense of Malcolm Little's experience of white racism by reference to a broad mythological and historical context was an important factor in his conversion.[297] There seems to be, however, no compelling reason why only Malcolm X's conversion should be explained by reference to such a broader context. The "Moonies" and the Apostles are parts of much wider worlds, as was Augustine of Hippo. Malcolm's interpretation of his own experience at least raises the possibility of other interpretive contexts for their conversions. It should be possible to trace both the influence of broader cultural and historical trends on individual conversions and the reciprocal and cumulative influence of numerous conversions on whole societies and cultures. To do so would be to seek a more general understanding of, for example, the rise of new religious movements in contemporary Europe and North America, the development of Christianity in the ancient Mediterranean world, or the historical advance of Christianity and Islam in Africa. To ask such questions is to move beyond the largely personal context of the first two chapters and the local social context of the third chapter and the opening pages of the fourth to broader social, cultural, and historical questions raised by conversion.

Stark and Bainbridge attempt to accomplish such a shift in focus by setting their treatment of new religious movements within the framework of certain general propositions about religion. They contend, for example, "that the sources of religion are shifting constantly in societies but that the amount of religion remains relatively constant."[298] They would thus reject out of hand any explanation of the rise of new religious movements that would link it to a quantitative increase in religious sentiment, the death rattle of traditional forms of religion, or to a pronounced increase in personal or social pathology. It cannot be clearly established that people were any more "spiritual" in the sixties than they were in the fifties or twenties. Long-established forms of Christianity and Judaism may hold less sway over American life, but rumours of their deaths are certainly premature and cannot provide a blanket explanation for conversion to new religious movements. Attempts to diagnose an entire generation are risky at best and cannot provide adequate scholarly explanations.

Instead of accepting any facile generalizations about conversion to new religions in the last quarter century, Stark and Bainbridge approach the problem by making a series of theoretical propositions about religion in general. They assert that processes of change are inherent within religion itself. They argue that as religious organizations come to include those who emphasize the otherworldly dimension along with those who stress the worldly dimension, a conflict of interest inevitably develops. Progressively stronger focus on the worldly dimension pushes in the direction of an accommodation with the world and gives impetus to the process of secularization. Since religions cannot serve both worldly and otherworldly interests equally well, those whose interests are not being served by accommodation with the world, those who are not gaining the rewards of the world and who are also paying most of the costs, will agitate for change. In its milder form change will lead to the formation of offshoots from the parent religious organization, sects which attempt to re-establish a sense of uneasiness with the world and re-direct the common focus to otherworldly dimensions. In its stronger form change will lead to the foundation of independent cults, which will seek members among those who have given up all organizational ties to the dominant religions. Thus, Stark and Bainbridge set the phenomena of conversion and the rise of new religions within a general portrait of how religious economies function. The process of secularization, or accommodation with the world, is the inherent dynamic which gives rise to two different movements, the formation of sects and cults. Each, in turn, when it becomes successful is subject to similar pressures to conform. Successful sects must face the dilemma of accomodating to the world all over again. Successful cults will also face a similar turning point.

Stark and Bainbridge's theory is intended to function on the most general level. It provides a theoretical account of the structure and function of religion and explains the phenomena of conversion and sect- and cult-formation within that account. It aims to answer questions about how religion, in a generic sense, "works." Though it could be adapted to other uses, it does not directly address specific questions of historical development within limited cultural areas. Jules-Rosette's brief treatment of the conversion of native Africans to the Church of John Maranke, however, suggests that such issues might be worth pursuing.

Both before and after her own conversion Jules-Rosette conducted over one humdred interviews with members of the Apostolic Church of John Maranke about the ways in which they became Apostles. In many interviews with men who held religious positions in the church she encountered primary explanations of conversion which, as should be expected, attributed it to divine activity. For example:

Q: Who gave you the news about this church?
R: The Holy Spirit itself showed me the Apostles praying in my house twice. Acts 9:3-6.
Q: Was this person an Apostle?
R: No, it was the Spirit of God.
Q: Why did you question him about the church?
R: No, I accepted abruptly because it is the Spirit of God.
Q: How did you feel at this time?
R: Because when the Spirit of God descended on me and chased the demons, I felt good. The sickness was over.
Q: When did this happen?

R: In 1971, when I was baptized.

Q: Why did you become a member of this church?

R: By the will of God. Jeremiah 31:3.[299]

Jules-Rosette's respondent recognizes no human agency in his conversion; it was the "Spirit of God," not any human Apostle, who gave him the news about John Maranke's church. That Spirit compels immediate acceptance, exorcizes demons, and heals sickness. It *acts upon* an essentially passive human subject. Male apostles do go on to exercise spiritual gifts and to play active roles in the affairs of the church, but they fairly consistently depict themselves as passive at the point of conversion.

The testimonies of female apostles, on the other hand, reveal more about the human and divine relationships involved in their conversions. They tend to have a different set of concerns; frequently mentioning "questions of faith healing, the alleviation of female disorders, and the mysticism of eternal life."[300] Their different interests lead female Apostles to favor different explanations of conversion. Interestingly, they make ample use of the image of the active self in describing their pre-conversion condition, their initial encounter with the church, and their decision to become members. The following exchange is representative:

Q: Who gave you the news about this church?

R: The first person that I saw was a mama. It was Mama Ngalula Ruth. Ngalula Ruth.

Q: What did she say?

R: She informed me about the church, that it was a good church. And first, since we have lots of cares, sickness, and frequent the hospital she said to us, that if you enter our church, all that you spend of silver and go take medicines, that has no importance, and you will see for yourself how God helps us.

Q: Was this person an Apostle?

R: She is an Apostle up to the present.

Q: When did this happen?

R: 'Seventy.

Q: How did you feel at this time?

R: At that time, my desire was to enter this church. If one dies in this church, I shall die too; if one stays alive, I shall stay alive.[301]

The respondent focuses on the direct agency of a woman within the Apostolic community who spreads the news about the church. She presents the church's teachings as an immediate and therapeutic response to her condition. Attracted by the possibility of "help" for her condition, the respondent decides to enter the church, aware of both the physical and metaphysical life that it promises her. The distinction between the female Apostles' use of the image of an active, decision-making self in their explanation of their conversion experiences and the male Apostles' reliance of an image of the passive self reinforces several observations made previously. The Apostles' answers show, as James would expect, the varieties of religious experience. They show also, as Proudfoot would expect, that the diversity of experience is directly linked to a diversity of primary explanations of that experience. They indicate as well that an image of the passive self is not a necessary component of primary descriptions and explanations of conversion, even within the same religious community and even if secondary and normative theological explanations would assert that it must be the case. Converts choose, explicitly or implicitly, to describe and explain their experience in certain ways. Such decisions are not made in isolation, but in the contexts of the historical experience and social circumstances of the individual convert. Those contexts leave an indelible mark on the experience as described and explained by the individual convert. Accordingly, the language that converts use to recount their experience is not secret and personal but public and accessible. Since that is the case, it then becomes possible for an outside observer to describe, analyze, and propose a secondary explanation of the convert's experience.[302]

Although Jules-Rosette initially uses her conversations with individual Apostles as evidence of the particular nature of the conversion experience, she also addresses questions about their broader significance in two ways. First, she notes the Apostles' attempt to manage ideological change. Jules-Rosette depicts Apostolic belief and practice as a transmutation of tradition that attempts to maintain "a subtle balancing of the relationship between custom and a vision of change."[303] Apostles will, for example, be careful to substitute Christian holy water for traditional herbal medicines; they attempt to respond to at least as wide a range of human needs and desires as the traditional religious system did. If anything, the Apostles tend to err in the direction of respect for tradition. Nonetheless, the Apostolic Church cuts across local, regional, and national boundaries, and the beliefs and practices common to all members therefore create a reality independent of specific tribal tradition. Second, conversion to the Apostolic Church is directly related to social change in central Africa. The apparent appeal of the Bapostolo to first generation city-dwellers, at least in Zaire, sets conversion to the Apostolic Church in the context of a general African trend towards urbanization. Jules-Rosette documents a sequence of events in which men move to cities seeking work and money; once there they convert; female family members later follow the men to the city, and the women themselves join the church once they arrive.[304] Jules-Rosette notes but does not specifically endorse an explanation which claims that the church offers a network of social relationships in the urban setting that substitutes for the tribal and familial ties ruptured by emigration.[305] She finds it difficult to determine whether the new urban patterns of relationships are primarily linked to the church. Instead, Jules-Rosette sees the urban setting and the church working together to replace traditional customs with more flexible ones. According to her, "the structure of kinship and of traditional communal life is reinterpreted and to a certain extent retained through Apostolic social organization."[306]

In the present context Jules-Rosette's specific explanation of the links between urban migration and membership in the Apostolic Church is less important than the set of issues her comments introduce. How is conversion to an independent Christian church, such as that of John Maranke, related to broader social and historical changes such as increasing urbanization, the introduction of Christianity (and Islam) into sub-Saharan Africa by traders, colonial administrators, and missionaries, and the whole complex of changes involved in modernization? Most observers of the growth of Christianity and Islam in Africa address those questions in at least an ad hoc way, but no one has done so in as consistent and provocative a fashion as Robin Horton.

Conversion in Africa

In a series of articles on "African Conversion," Horton has developed a comprehensive answer to "the question of the causes of conversion from 'traditional' to 'world' religions."[307] At the center of his argument is a fascinating "thought-experiment." Horton attempts to describe the hypothetical development of traditional African religions under the impact of the various forces of modernization, *minus* the influence of Christianity and Islam. In Africa, Horton notes, "Christianity itself came to be seen as part of a larger order, comprising Western education, colonial administration, commerce and industry."[308] He proposes simply to extract Christianity and Islam from that complex of factors and to imagine what the consequences would have been. At the conclusion of his experiment Horton contends

> The obvious inference is that acceptance of Islam and Christianity is due as much to development of the traditional cosmology in response to *other* features of the modern situation as it is to the activities of the missionaries.[309]

The process by which Horton arrives at that judgment is worth considering in detail.

Horton's argument depends both on a series of generalizations and on a particular theoretical stance. His primary generalization is his synthetic portrait of a generic, traditional African cosmology. The traditional cosmology divides the realm of supernatural entities into two tiers: that of the lesser spirits who are concerned with the affairs of the local community, and that of the high god who is concerned with the world as a whole. Noting the lack of attention directed to the supreme being and the correspondingly greater attention directed to the lesser spirits in traditional societies, Horton explains them as a function of the social experience and horizons of the individual:

> The essence of the pre-modern situation is that most events affecting the life of the individual occur within the microcosm of the local community, and that this microcosm is to a considerable extent insulated from the macrocosm of the wider world. Since most significant interaction occurs within the local community, moral rules tend to apply within this community rather than universally . . . .[310]

That formulation of the relationship between social experience and belief allows Horton to predict that a weakening of the boundaries of the local community will precipitate greater interest in the supreme being whose primary realm of concern is the macrocosm. On a large scale:

> If thousands of people find themselves outside the microcosm, and if even those left inside see the boundaries weakening if not actually dissolving, they can only interpret these changes by assuming that the lesser spirits (underpinners of the microcosms) are in retreat, and that the supreme being (underpinner of the macrocosm) is taking over direct control of the everyday world.[311]

Consequently, Horton can interpret increased conversion to Christianity and Islam in Africa as being directly related to the historical weakening of local communities and the consequent entrance of individuals into a social world of much broader horizons. That is, for example, just the sort of change experienced by Jules-Rosette's first generation city-dwellers who became members of the Apostolic Church of John Maranke. Horton would explain their adoption of Christianity as being directly related to the disruption of family and tribal ties caused by emigration to the city. He might suggest further that the Apostles' attempt to maintain a balance between traditional and innovative beliefs and practices must inevitably tip in favor of the new, unless the Apostles take specific action to preserve tradition. That some Apostles continue to take up residence periodically in their rural home villages could be construed as reinforcing the hold of traditional beliefs.[312]

Horton's thought-experiment places Christianity and Islam in the role of catalysts or "stimulators and accelerators of changes which were 'in the air' anyway."[313] It explains, he contends, why some Africans embraced Christianity and Islam, why they accepted and failed to accept particular elements of each tradition, why some converts retained certain elements of traditional belief and practice, and why some failed to convert at all. Horton proposes this guideline: "the beliefs and practices of the so-called world religions are only accepted where they happen to coincide with responses of the traditional cosmology to other, non-missionary, factors of the modern situation."[314] Accordingly, those most involved with the macrocosm, the broader society of region or nation, will be most likely to devote their religious attention to the supreme deity, while those who remain most securely within the bounds of the local community will be least likely to do so. Individual conversions to Christianity or Islam become, in Horton's interpretation, merely the tip of the iceberg. For him, the full impact of conversion can not be adequately explained as a personal experience, as the act of God, or as the result of social interaction with friends or new acquaintances. Proper understanding of conversion to world religions in Africa, at least, demands a sweeping overview of cultural history. The "causes" of such conversion are not to be located either solely within the individual or within the activities of formal or informal proselytizers in the local context. Missionary and convert alike are caught up in a greater, more complex process.

Horton describes that process specifically as an *interpretive* one. In general, he views "recent developments in African belief and ritual as responses of the traditional cosmology to the successive interpretative challenges posed by modern social change."[315] It is more difficult to conceive of interpretation primarily as something that *happens to* someone than it is to think of it as something that someone *does*. Horton's explanation of conversion explicitly depends upon an image of the active, decision-making self. Horton describes his theoretical stance as an "intellectualist" approach, acknowledging a specific debt to E. B. Tylor. In conscious distinction to anthropologists who view traditional beliefs and practices as expressive or symbolic of some other reality, "the intellectualist approach . . . takes systems of traditional religious belief at their face value—i.e. as theoretical systems intended for the explanation, prediction, and control of space-time events."[316] From that perspective the significance of conversion is that it reveals "a people struggling to adapt its stock of theoretical concepts to the explanation, prediction, and control of events in a new and unfamiliar social situation."[317] Such an approach puts the image of the active self to vigorous use. It suggests that any inquiry into religion should begin by examining stated beliefs in terms of the explicit explanatory ends they serve.[318] Such an emphasis is compatible with the discussion in the previous chapters of how explanatory claims appear to be embedded in descriptions of religious experience; it directs attention first to what I have called primary explanations but also to some types of secondary explanations (e.g. theological ones) as well.

The intellectualist approach holds that traditional religious beliefs are explanatory in intent, even if they can be shown to be wrong according to the canons of modern Western science. Such beliefs are primarily concerned with the explanation, prediction, and control of events within the local community. Religion, in that view, can be described as the extension of social relations beyond the confines of strictly human society and into the realm of supernatural beings.[319] In religion people interact with spirits and gods as if the supernatural beings were themselves people; the world of religious people includes invisible but personal forces. Accordingly, the types of relationships they can have with spirits or gods will be modeled on the types of relationships they actually do have with their fellow human beings.

The impact of Horton's intellectualist theory of religion on his interpretation of conversion to Christianity and Islam in Africa can be easily detailed. Horton's starting point is the typical traditional cosmology; the crucial variables will be the pre-existent patterns of thought rather than any external influences.[320] Accordingly, where there is no radical change in cosmology, it will be doubtful that conversion has occurred.[321] When a change in cosmology does occur, its cause should be sought less in individual experience or in local social interaction than in the underlying cultural changes promoted by the cluster of processes that constitute modern social change. Conversions to Christianity and Islam should be considered "responses which, given the appropriate economic and social background conditions, would most likely have occurred in some recognizable form even in the absence of the world religions."[322] Horton thus blends an appreciation of the active self, with its search to make sense of change in terms of traditional views of the world, with a recognition of the powerful influence of long-term cultural and social trends. Admittedly, he focuses much more on the characterization of such long-term change, but that is precisely his theoretical point; interpretations of African conversions to world religions that focus on the personal or the local social context inevitably will miss the crucial explanatory elements.

Horton's work has drawn criticism both for its treatment of specific data and for its theoretical position. He, in turn, has seized the opportunity to respond and to clarify his argument. Because the challenges to Horton's theoretical stance will be more instructive for the understanding of conversion, disputes about particular points of African religious history will be left to the side here. Horton sees in some of his opponents the not unlikely combination of a strong religious commitment and an obdurate refusal to accept causal explanations of religious beliefs and practices. He claims that those two positions are linked by "the premise that statements about the causes of beliefs have negative implications for the truth-values of those beliefs."[323] The rejection of causal explanation is often linked to the assertion of the autonomy of religious experience and belief and their *sui generis* nature. Proudfoot claims that such a description of religion "has become the chief strategy for protecting religious beliefs and practices from the possibility of conflict with the conclusions of science or with the assumptions that inform our perceptual and moral experience."[324] Horton, in addition, finds it ironic that those who would preserve and protect religion from criticism end up accepting the premise of their opponents who, like Durkheim and Freud, believe that by identifying the causes of religious belief they could loosen its hold on human beings. In Horton's view the intellectualist search for the causes of conversion to Christianity and Islam in Africa has no necessary consequences for the truth or falsity of Christian and Muslim beliefs. It is simply the most adequate way of arriving at a comprehensive explanation. Proudfoot's distinction between descriptive and explanatory reduction is helpful here. He writes that "*Descriptive reduction* is the failure to identify an emotion, practice, or experience under the description by which the subject identifies it."[325] Horton would agree about the unacceptability of that procedure; he provides full descriptions of the conversion phenomena under consideration. On the other hand, "*Explanatory reduction* consists in offering an explanation of an experience in terms that are not those of the subject and that might not meet with his approval."[326] That is precisely what Horton has done by explaining conversion to Christianity and Islam in Africa by reference to the broader currents of modernization. The critics he describes as "the Devout Opposition" will only accept an explanation phrased in terms acceptable to the religious subjects. That would, however, unnecessarily limit the explanatory task to the repetition and amplification of subjects' primary explanations of their own behavior. As I have shown in the previous chapters, relying on some of the distinctions proposed by Proudfoot, that is only one of the forms that secondary explanations may take.

The second criticism of Horton's intellectualist approach should be familiar from the discussion of Lofland and Stark's "Becoming a World-Saver" in the previous chapter. That criticism holds that the intellectualist characterization of religions as systems of thought and meaning ignores their social dimensions. Horton's response succinctly states his position:

> . . . cosmology, and its related cultic practice, arises as a response to *experience*. We do maintain that religions must be regarded first and foremost as systems of thought; but experience, not thought, is the object of thought and hence of religion. And as sociologists we are concerned with thought as a response to social experience.[327]

It hardly needs to be stated that Horton would not consider experience to be immune to the influences of social life. The intellectualist approach looks to thinking individuals in their appropriate social and historical contexts.

Horton offers an example of the integration of personal experience, individual deliberation, social context and historical development into a coherent explanation of the conversion of native Africans to Christianity and Islam. He thus raises questions that move beyond the personal and local contexts of conversion and toward a consideration of its historical significance. By arguing not that Christianity and Islam have transformed the face of Africa, but that they have participated in and, on occasion, catalyzed the transformation, Horton steers between elevating religion to a position of unique and independent importance in human life and a dismissal of it as a factor of no importance.

Conclusions

I have used the African material in this chapter to raise several questions. Initially, I used Jules-Rosette's description and explanation of her own conversion to test Lofland's suspicion that more attention should be directed to "how people go about converting themselves." I have suggested further that such a focus will yield explanations which depend on an image of the active, decision-making, self. My distinction between the images of the active and passive self, however, differs from James' distinction between conversion by volition and by self-surrender by focusing on *explanation* rather than *experience*.

I have also argued that most explanations of conversion focus either on the *personal* or *local* context of the transformation of the self. Jules-Rosette's attempt to relate conversion to the Church of John Maranke to needs of first generation city-dwellers in central Africa introduced the possibility of much broader contexts of explanation. No one one has argued the case for such explanations more forcefully than Robin Horton. For him, conversion to Christianity and Islam in Africa can only be read against the long history of cultural and historical changes that has produced the current situation. Horton's theoretical approach to, and specific characterization of, that situation have both been disputed. Horton is most important here, however, for raising the issue in a clear and persuasive manner.

In the chapter that follows I will take up the question of the historical significance of conversion to Christianity in a different time period and cultural area. The transformation of Christianity from an obscure Palestinian sect to the dominant religion of the Roman world in the space of three centuries has long taxed the imaginations of historians. The phenomenon of conversion is central to the question. How and why did Christianity gain so many adherents so quickly? As is the case with Islam and Christianity in Africa, many different answers have been proposed.

Understanding Conversion in Late Antiquity

At least one study has drawn attention to the similarities between conversion to Christianity and Islam in modern Africa and the initial growth of Christianity in the ancient Mediterranean world. In characterizing the "underlying pattern" of the history of Islam in Africa as one of successive stages of "quarantine, mixing, and reform," Humphrey J. Fisher relies on Arthur Darby Nock's *Conversion* for analytical categories and an example of the career of a prophetic religion. Fisher applies to Islam Nock's distinction between prophetic religions, which demand conversion of the individual, and traditional religions, which demand only adhesion. He observes that "what is peculiar to the situation in tropical Africa is that, while Islam is a prophetic religion, theoretically demanding conversion, it is very often regarded in practice, in its mixed form in Africa, as a non-prophetic one, for which adhesion is entirely adequate."[328] Fisher also follows Nock in identifying "two distinct crises of religious development: exchanging one faith (or none) for another, and exchanging indifference and dilution for fervency within the same faith."[329] He argues further that specific understandings of conversion are more appropriate to one rather than another stage in the history of African Islam. For example, conversion as a change from casual adherence to fervent faith would characterize the reform phase, while conversion as a change from one faith to another would characterize the initial quarantine phase. In the quarantine and reform phases Islam might well appear as a prophetic religion, but in its mixing phase it is much less so. Rather than any specific comparisons of African Muslim and ancient Christian converts, Nock's analytical categories and the general pattern of development that he describes are what Fisher finds useful for charting the history of Islam in Africa.

Fisher also criticizes Robin Horton for focusing only

on the first type of conversion and thus misconstruing "the esential, underlying movement of religious growth" in Africa. Though Horton responded with a vigorous and detailed defense of his intellectualist explanation of African conversion, what is of interest here is Fisher's adaptation of Nock's explanation of one instance of historical change to the explanation of another. Fisher treats conversion first as a generic religious phenomenon and thus as a proper subject for theoretical arguments developed on the basis of other data, and second, as a phenomenon with particular historical, cultural, and religious dimensions. As a result, he asserts that instructive comparisons can be made between the rise of Christianity in the ancient Mediterranean world and the growth of Islam in sub-Saharan Africa. In each instance conversion is considered as an element in a broader and more complex process of historical change. I have already considered that process in Africa in the previous chapter. In this chapter I turn, with Fisher and Nock, to the ancient Mediterranean.

Nock's Theory of Conversion

In *Conversion: The Old and the New in Religion from Alexander the Great to Augustine of Hippo*, Nock's primary concern is the growth of Christianity. He acknowledges, however, that "we cannot understand the success of Christianity outside Judaea without making an effort to determine the elements in the mind of the time to which it appealed."[330] That psychologized description of a historical problem captures Nock's twin interests in juxtaposition. On the one hand, he is interested in describing a complex of changes in ancient religious life that unfolded over a period of several centuries. On the other, he sees those changes as being largely psychological, changes of mind. Both interests will be in evidence as Nock moves from general accounts of the progress of "eastern cults" in the Roman empire to specific studies of exemplary figures, such as Lucius in Apuleius' *Golden Ass* or Augustine of Hippo.

Nock begins with a sketch of the traditional Greek religion of the *polis* in the period before Alexander as background for the religious changes of the Hellenistic and Roman periods. He then describes the success of such new or newly transformed religions as the cults of Isis, Mithras, Dionysos, and Cybele as a prominent characteristic of the religious climate and social situation into which Christianity enters. For Nock, conversion to Christianity has to be understood as a distinctive act in the much larger pageant of religious life in the Roman Empire. What distinguishes early Christianity from most of the other religions at the time is its insistence upon conversion. Christianity made exclusive claims on an individual's religious loyalty. A Christian could not, for example, participate in both the worship of Isis and the Lord's Supper. Christian converts, as the early Christian missionary Paul puts it, had turned "from idols, to serve a living and true God."[331] To turn back again or to attempt to serve both would be to invite peril. Nock asserts that in the ancient world only Judaism, and to some extent philosophy, drew such sharp boundaries between mutually exclusive ways of life.

Nock's picture of the "religious economy" of the Roman world expresses as well his general theoretical understanding of religion. For Nock, religion addresses mysteries that seem beyond the mastery of human beings, such as the cycle of life from birth through death, the pursuit of sustenance through hunting and agriculture, or "the secret workings of nature."[332] The human attempts to understand and to act appropriately towards such mysteries constitute religion. As a result, religion has both psychological and sociological aspects. On the one hand, it involves "making vocal many of the impulses which lie below the level of consciousness and producing a delicate interplay between them and the intellect;" while on the other, it can manifest either "group solidarity" or "emergent individualism," depending on the context.[333]

Left to themselves, religious people "have no reason to interest themselves in other traditions, and no impulse to commend their own tradition to others. It serves their own needs, and the members of other social units have traditions which serve theirs."[334] In such circumstances religions change only gradually, "unless new needs or new cultural contacts arise."[335] Religious change could thus be prompted by trade, travel, or more violent forms of cultural interchange, such as invasion or conquest. For Nock, however, the most thorough and dramatic form of religious change is that provoked by a prophet "who experiences a sudden and profound dissatisfaction with things as they are."[336] Prophetic preaching poses for the individual a stark choice between embracing the proclaimed future and retaining the familiar past. By identifying problems and their solutions, by stirring up a sense of uneasiness and then describing how it can be resolved, prophets, prophetic movements, and prophetic religions create the needs which they then claim to fulfill.[337] The prophet sets into motion a chain of events which can proceed from the initial attraction of followers, through their proselytizing and the growth of the movement, to the formation of an institution. In time, the institution itself may become subject to new prophetic criticism, thus beginning the cycle again.

Prophets, prophetic movements, and prophetic religions all demand conversion, not adhesion. They offer a new life, which can only be pursued if the old life is left totally behind. They claim the whole human being. In Nock's words, they seek

> the reorientation of the soul of an individual,
> his deliberate turning from indifference or from
> an earlier form of piety to another, a turning
> which implies a consciousness that a greater
> change is involved, that the old was wrong and
> the new is right.[338]

That understanding of conversion derives directly from William James' exposition in *The Varieties*. Nock explicitly follows James in identifying the features of conversion as "a passion of willingness and acquiescence, which removes the feeling of anxiety, a sense of perceiving truths not known before, a sense of clean and beautiful newness within and without and an ecstasy of happiness."[339] For Nock, as for James, conversion involves "a turning away from a sense of present wrongness" to a "positive ideal."[340]

In adopting James' understanding of conversion, Nock implicitly adopts his theory of religion as well. Even in his definition of the two types of religion, Nock recapitulates James' interest in those individuals whose religion is first-hand and white hot by focusing on the definitive role of the prophet. Nock even employs metaphorical language similar to James' when he describes the prophet's "ability to fuse into a white heat combustible material which is there, to express and to appear to meet the half-formed prayers of some at least of his contemporaries."[341] James' influence also becomes evident when Nock turns from his general account of the diffusion and success of new religious cults in the Roman empire to his specific discussion of conversion to

Christianity. As in *The Varieties*, although not to the same extent, the testimonies of specific individuals provide the crucial evidence.

Given James' dismissal of ritual, doctrine, and community organization as second-hand manifestations of religion, it is questionable whether a discussion of the growth of ancient Christianity which depends on James' theory of religion is adequate to the task. The attempt to tell the story of the rise of Christianity primarily through a focus on the exaggerated cases of a few religious virtuosos risks leaving out other important factors. It also remains to be seen whether James' interest in the phenomenon and process of conversion be blended with Nock's more historical question about the reasons behind the success of Christianity in the ancient world. The question Nock poses is clear enough, but it is not certain that he has chosen the appropriate tools for the task of answering it. It will be helpful at this point to review Nock's intentions and to assess his accomplishments.

Nock intends to make several points. In general, they involve separating Christianity out from the welter of competing religions and proposing an explanation for its singular success. The significance of that success for the history of the ancient world remains in the background. Nock first wants to demonstrate the accuracy of distinguishing between the conversion demanded by Judaism, Christianity, and certain forms of philosophy and the mere adhesion required by all other religions in the Roman world. He then wants to offer an explanation of the extraordinary success of Christianity, which far surpassed Judaism and philosophy in attracting a large number of converts. That, in turn, will lead to a clearer understanding of how Christianity contributed to the transformation of the ancient world. In what follows I will re-examine some of Nock's examples and introduce a few of my own in order to establish whether the distinctions he made and the conclusions he drew can be upheld. I will concentrate on texts which can be dated, with more or less certainty, to the second century of the common era.

Perhaps the crucial element in Nock's definition is that conversion entails the conviction that "the old was wrong and the new is right." In contrast, adhesion would describe a conviction that the old was right and still is right, or that the old was right and the new is right, too. Conversion, for Nock, implies a conscious decision to reject the past and accept a new future;

adhesion implies a continuing acceptance of the past, either by itself or in combination with something new. Such "a consciousness that a great change is involved" marks the testimonies of converts to philosophy, Judaism, and Christianity alike.

Conversion in Late Antiquity

The second-century satirist Lucian (c. 120-180 C.E.), from Samosata on the banks of the Euphrates, is best known for his deft skewering of religious and philosophical pretentiousness, credulity, and confusion. He was, however, like all satirists, not without his own convictions. In a brief text that seems to preserve some autobiographical details he describes how he deserted rhetoric for philosophy, inspired by his encounter with the Platonist philosopher "Nigrinus."[342]

Lucian begins with a letter to Nigrinus in which he declares that he wishes to reveal his state of mind, specifically because he has been so moved by Nigrinus' teaching. There follows a dialogue between Lucian and an unidentified interlocutor that chronicles Lucian's trip to Rome, encounter with Nigrinus, and return home. The interlocutor sets the tone for the discussion by noting that Lucian seems to "have changed all of a sudden."[343] Lucian's reply confirms his suspicions with a question shot through with images of conversion that recall "Amazing Grace":

> Don't you think it wonderful, in the name of Zeus, that once a slave, I am now free! "once poor, now rich indeed;" once witless and befogged, now saner?[344]

He then quickly recounts his descent into confusion at his initial conversation with Nigrinus and his rapid emergence into a clarity of philosophical vision and rejection of his past attachment to wealth, power, and reputation.[345] Lucian uses a variety of images to conjure up his transformation: he "grew sharper-sighted in [his] soul";[346] he is "going about enraptured and drunk with the wine of his discourse";[347] he is "in the same case with lovers";[348] he looks at Nigrinus as if "he were a lighthouse and I were adrift at sea in the dead of night."[349] All of those images are designed to evoke the sudden change of which Lucian has become conscious.

By condemning his past and extolling his present, Lucian fits Nock's definition of the convert who reaches the conclusion "that the old was wrong and the new is right." He also would fit James' description of a process in which religious (or, in this case, philosophical) interests that were once peripheral to him now occupy the center of his energy. Lucian has certainly changed his mind, and that change leads him to act differently, especially in regard to issues of wealth, power, and reputation. Even if Lucian doesn't join a community of the like-minded, the way he behaves in the world is, he tells us, permanently altered by his encounter with Nigrinus. Like the prophet's disciples described by Nock, Lucian also becomes so eager in his espousal of Nigrinus' teaching that he seeks to convey the truth he has found to others.[350]

Lucian's impassioned testimony successfully piques his listener's interest:

> I should like to hear just what he [Nigrinus] said, if possible. It is far, very far from right, in my opinion, to be stingy with it, especially if the person who wants to hear is a friend and has the same interests.[351]

That eager declaration of sympathy declares the interlocutor's openness and leaves him poised to act should the wisdom of Nigrinus live up to Lucian's enthusiastic praise.

As it is revealed in the major portion of the dialogue, that wisdom consists of brief anecdotes which illustrate the Athenian philosopher's scorn for ostentatious luxury[352] and praise for the philosophical life of poverty;[353] an account of Nigrinus' own decision to "imitate Odysseus" and sail past the desires which assail human beings;[354] an extensive criticism of the rich and those who live off their wealth, particularly philosophers;[355] an account of how Nigrinus embodied those criticisms in his own life;[356] and a final indictment of the various follies of humankind.[357] Lucian again testifies that he was "spellbound" by that teaching. In a scene reminiscent of Augustine's moments of torment in the garden at Milan, Lucian recalls that he was so emotionally moved that

> in a great fit of confusion and giddiness, I dripped with sweat, I stumbled and stuck in the endeavour to speak, my voice failed, my

tongued faltered, and finally I began to cry in
embarrassment; for the effect he produced in
me was not superficial or casual. My wound
was deep and vital, and his words, shot with
great accuracy, love, if I may say so, my very
soul in twain.[358]

Like Stephen Bradley, Lucian attributes his physical
symptoms to a specific cause; he offers an explanation of
his own experience. Lucian does not attribute his
conversion to the miraculous intervention of the Christian Holy Spirit or to the sing-song command of a
disembodied voice; rather he attributes it to his
immensely profitable encounter with a man of wisdom.
He notes, however, just as Nock and James observe,[359]
that a prior receptivity is a necessity:

not all who listen to philosophers go away
enraptured and wounded, but only those who
previously had in their nature some secret bond
of kinship with philosophy.[360]

That description of what predisposes some people
towards conversion recalls the interlocutor's earlier
remark that he shares with Lucian "the same interests."[361] It comes as no surprise, then, that at the close
of Lucian's tale the interlocutor reports that as Lucian
spoke he "felt something like a change of heart."[362] He,
too, is now "wounded" by the words of Nigrinus and
the example of Lucian's conversion to philosophy. The
dialogue ends with their joint resolve to return to the
man who wounded them to seek "healing." In Lofland
and Stark's terms, in the dialogue that he records Lucian
has acted successfully as a "deployable agent" on behalf
of Nigrinus' philosophy.

The interlocutor's conversion becomes the final link in
a chain of imitation that stretches back to Homer. Just
as Nigrinus claims that he will "imitate Odysseus"[363] in
sailing by the attractive pleasures of life, so also does
Lucian describe him as a model in his contempt for
wealth[364] and "in his simple diet, his moderate physical
exercises, his earnest face, his plain clothes, and above
all, his well-balanced understanding and his kindly
ways."[365] As Lucian describes his own transformation, it
becomes clear that he has taken Nigrinus' teaching and
example to heart. The evident metamorphosis of Lucian
into "a happy and blessed man"[366] provokes first the
interest, then the sympathy, and finally the imitation of
his interlocutor. In that final case, Nigrinus' teaching is
mediated through Lucian's description of the effect it

had on him. For the interlocutor, Lucian embodies the teaching of Nigrinus. To accept the teaching is to imitate Lucian, who in turn imitates the master.

Conversion to philosophy, in *The Wisdom of Nigrinus*, is portrayed as a definite break with the past. In renouncing the trifling attractions of the world, the philosophical convert joins not a specific social group but a community of the wise that transcends time and place. Such conversion is clearly "the reorientation of the soul of an individual"; in a sense, it is a change of world view. That change of perspective also has concrete effects: the philosophical convert no longer seeks "wealth and reputation, dominion and honour, yes and purple and gold."[367] If such a movement into philosophy can, according to Nock's criteria, be classified as a conversion, it will be important to ask further about the ways in which it is similar to and different from conversion to Christianity.

The Christian teacher Justin offers an interesting point of comparison. Born around the turn of the second century at Nablus in Samaria to a pagan family of Roman colonists, he became a Christian sometime around the year 130 C.E., some thirty years before Lucian's conversion to Platonic philosophy. Justin died, a martyr for his faith, around the year 165 C.E. During his career as a Christian teacher Justin produced several apologetic works. He opens one of them, the *Dialogue with Trypho*, with what may be a rather stylized account of his own conversion.[368]

Like Lucian, Justin was attracted by philosophy. But he was not so fortunate as to acquire satisfying wisdom in his initial encounter. His spiritual life, like that of Augustine in chapter two and like those of the Moonies and former Moonies in chapter three, was a prolonged quest for wisdom. Like other seekers in Late Antiquity, Justin made the rounds of the philosophical schools in his search for wisdom. He weaves the story of that search into the opening chapters of his *Dialogue with Trypho*. The story is probably set in the town of Ephesus on the west coast of Asia Minor.[369] While Justin is out walking the streets of the city, he encounters a stranger who identifies him by his garb as a philosopher and engages him in conversation. The stranger identifies himself as Trypho, a Jew who is currently a resident of Corinth in Greece. Justin expresses some surprise at the Jew's interest in philosophy:

"How," I asked, "can you gain as much from

> philosophy as from your own lawgiver and
> prophets?"

> "Why not," he replied, "for do not the philoso-
> phers speak always about God? Do they not
> constantly propose questions about his unity
> and providence? Is this not the task of
> philosophy, to inquire about the Divine?"[370]

Justin acknowledges that he, too, is of the same opinion.
With that the topic of the conversation and, as it will
turn out, the nature of Justin's conversion to Christianity
is clearly indicated. Moses, the prophets, and the
philosophers share a common object of inquiry, "the
Divine." In that view, the realms of philosophy and
religion overlap, if they are not identical. Questions
about the views of Moses and the Hebrew prophets will
be philosophical questions, just as questions about the
views of philosophers will be religious questions.

Though Justin and Trypho quickly discover their
common interest in philosophy, it takes some time for
Justin to recount the story of his conversion to Christianity. Justin first tells of his extended search through
the various schools for the true philosophy. Convinced
that "philosophy is indeed one's greatest possession, and
is most precious in the sight of God, to whom it alone
leads us and to whom it unites us,"[371] Justin sought
wisdom first from a Stoic, then a Peripatetic and a
Pythagorean, and finally from the Platonists. In each
case he was disappointed in his quest for a vision of
God.[372] Frustrated in his desires and agitated in his
mind, Justin used to walk the beach. One day, he
encountered with an old man there who began a
conversation with him about the philosophical search for
God:

> "Then how," he reasoned, "can the philoso-
> phers speculate correctly or speak truly of God,
> when they have no knowledge of Him, since
> they have never seen nor heard Him?"

> "But the deity, father," I rejoined, "cannot be
> seen by the same eyes as other living beings
> are. He is to be perceived by the mind alone,
> as Plato affirms, and I agree with him."[373]

The old man's questioning eventually shakes Justin's
confidence in the truth of Platonic philosophy. When
Justin expresses his confusion, he is offered an
alternative:

> "If these philosophers," I asked, "do not know

the truth, what teacher or method shall one follow?"

"A long time ago," he replied, "long before the time of those reputed philosophers, there lived blessed men who were just and loved by God, men who spoke through the inspiration of the Holy Spirit and predicted events that would take place in the future, which events are now taking place. We call these men the Prophets. They alone knew the truth and communicated it to men. . . . Their writings are still extant, and whoever reads them with the proper faith will profit greatly in his knowledge of the origin and end of things, and of any other matter that a philosopher should know.[374]

Justin reports that as the old man was speaking "my spirit was immediately set on fire, and an affection for the prophets, and for those who are friends of Christ, took hold of me; while pondering on his words, I discovered that this was the only sure and useful philosophy."[375] His conversion culminates with this declaration: "Thus it is that I am now a philosopher."[376] Since it is perfectly clear that Justin has become a Christian, his choice of words is particularly telling. For Justin, Christianity is the true philosophy. He finds in it the goal of his quest for philosophical wisdom.

Within the context of the frame story of the *Dialogue*, Justin hopes to make his own conversion to Christianity intelligible to Trypho and to make it seem the kind of thing that a sincere philosopher might typically do. At the end of the account of his conversion Justin makes the plea to Trypho explicit: "Thus if you have any regard for your own welfare and for the salvation of your soul and if you believe in God you may have this chance, since I know you are no stranger to this matter, of attaining a knowledge of the Christ of God, and, after becoming a Christian, of enjoying a happy life."[377] That comment shows that Justin recognizes other dimensions of his new faith; it enables the convert to lead a happy life on earth and to secure salvation of the soul after death. As might be expected, Trypho rejects Justin's plea for his conversion. The rest of the *Dialogue* resolves into an extended debate about whether the Jewish or Christian position represents the proper understanding of the Hebrew Bible, a question which does not have direct bearing on the topic at hand.

Justin has obviously converted, in Nock's sense. He embraces in Christianity "the only sure and useful philosophy." The note of exclusiveness is clear; like Lucian, Justin has changed his mind. Justin's conversion, however, is more than a change in world view. Justin's comments in another of his works display the cosmic, moral, and social dimensions of Christian conversion:

> . . . we, also, after our conversion by the Word have separated ourselves from those demons and have attached ourselves to the only unbegotten God, through His Son. We who once reveled in impurities, now cling to purity; we who devoted ourselves to the arts of magic now consecrate ourselves to the good and unbegotten God; we who loved above all else the ways of acquiring riches and possessions now hand over to a community fund what we possess, and share it with every needy person; we who hated and killed one another and would not share our hearth with those of another tribe because of their [different] customs, now, after the coming of Christ, live together with them, and pray for our enemies, and try to convince those who hate us unjustly, so that they who live according to the good commands of Christ may have a firm hope of receiving the same reward as ourselves from God who governs all.[378]

In language more complex than the first verse of "Amazing Grace" or Lucian's simple assertion that he had been a slave but that he attained freedom through philosophy, Justin carefully delineates the differences between the Christian's life before and after conversion. If Justin tends to identify Christianity and philosophy, he does not take a narrow view of what accepting that philosophy entails.

Justin certainly fits most profiles of the convert, and Nock uses him as an example of one of the three, very loosely defined, types of conversion to Christianity.[379] Justin's explanation of his own conversion, however, raises broader questions. In identifying his conversion as a conversion to philosophy, Justin gives no indication that he has proposed a novel understanding of his new religion. He assumes that what he has said will make sense. Nonetheless, it is possible to see that his conversion *to* Christianity is also indicative of the conversion *of* Christianity that began in the second century and continued in the third and fourth. Justin provides an example of the influx of intellectuals into

Christian communities. Relatively well-versed in ancient culture, they undertook, among other tasks, the systematic presentation of Christianity as religion that could make sense to an educated public. Whether such apologetic efforts actually provoked any conversions to the new religion is highly doubtful, but they did, it is clear, have the effect of reinforcing faith within the community by demonstrating its acceptibility and attractiveness on the basis of current standards.[380] It is thus possible to move beyond the details of Justin's conversion story to a consideration of the broader impact of the conversion of such educated and philosophically inclined individuals on the history of Christianity. It may not be an exaggeration to claim that they changed Christianity, or at least its public face in intellectual circles, as much as it changed them. The conversion in the second century of figures like Justin, Tatian, Theophilus, and Tertullian added to Christianity a corps of writers with significant intellectual abilities. In their books and in their work as teachers they are working out a Christian view of, and attitude toward, the surrounding world. While the conversion of a few intellectuals may not be numerically significant, their work had a broader impact. Justin's explanation of his own conversion as a conversion to philosophy signals that impact. I will return to that broader question after a brief discussion of conversion to Judaism and to other cults in Late Antiquity.

It is much more difficult to find even quasi-autobiographical accounts of conversion to Judaism in the second century. The material in the Mishnah (codified at the end of the second century) and later rabbinic sources has more to say about the opinions of various Jewish authorities than about the motives and experiences of converts themselves. The first-century authors Philo and Josephus provide scattered reports of conversions and some other relevant material.[381] For some indication of the understanding of conversion in certain Jewish circles I will turn to a text which is clearly a fiction. Nonetheless, the conversion that it attributes to its main character may still be instructive.

The romance of *Joseph and Aseneth* is an imaginative expansion of a few scenes from the biblical story of Joseph in Genesis 37-50.[382] It is likely to have been composed in Greek sometime between the first century before the common era and the second century after. It seems to come from a Judaism that was at home in the Greco-Roman world, though one that differed in recognizable ways with the Judaism of the Pharisees, Sadducees, Essenes, and other groups. The immediately relevant portion of the story concerns Joseph's encounter with Aseneth, the lovely and chaste daughter of an Egyptian nobleman; her father's attempt to arrange a marriage between her and Joseph; Aseneth's initial reluctance to marry and Joseph's fear that she will molest him; her repentence and conversion to the worship of the "God of Joseph"; and their eventual marriage. Aseneth is portrayed throughout the text as inherently sober and chaste, but her formal conversion to Judaism is necessary before her marriage can take place. In a sense *Joseph and Aseneth* responds to a question implicit in the Genesis story: how could Joseph have married an Egyptian woman?

At their first meeting Joseph's very appearance banishes Aseneth's fears about his immoral intentions. She is immediately impressed:

> And when Aseneth saw Joseph on his chariot and was strongly cut (to the heart), and her soul was crushed, and her knees were paralyzed, and her entire body trembled, and she was filled with great fear. And she sighed and said in her heart: . . .

> But I, foolish and daring, have despised him and spoken wicked words about him, and did not know that Joseph is (a) son of God.[383]

On his part, Joseph refuses even to kiss the young maiden because she is a heathen:

> It is not fitting for a man who worships God, who will bless with his mouth the living God and eat blessed bread of life and drink a blessed cup of immortality and anoint himself with blessed ointment of incorruptibility to kiss a strange woman who will bless with her mouth dead and dumb idols and eat from their table bread of strangulation and drink from their libation a cup of insidiousness and anoint herself with ointment of destruction.[384]

Joseph then prays that Aseneth will turn to the living and true God, making clear to Aseneth the choice that confronts her. As in the cases of so many other converts, Aseneth's spiritual crisis manifests itself in physical symptoms. In fear and trembling and total exhaustion, "she wept with great and bitter weeping and repented of her (infatuation with the) gods whom she

used to worship, and spurned all the idols."[385] Aseneth
then throws away her jewelry, cosmetics, other finery,
and the gold and silver representations of her former
gods. She puts on mourning clothes and begins a seven
day fast. Through many such concrete acts Aseneth cuts
herself off from her past, even to the extent that she can
imagine her parents refusing to acknowledge that she is
their daughter.[386] In an extended soliloquy, she surrenders herself to her new God:

> With you I take refuge, Lord,
> and to you I will shout, Lord,
> to you I will pour out my supplication,
> to you I will confess my sins,
> and to you I will reveal my lawless deeds.
> Spare me, Lord
> because I have sinned much before you,
> I have committed lawlesness and irreverence,
> and have said wicked and unspeakable (things)
> before you.[387]

Aseneth's confession is followed by a vision of a
heavenly figure who promises her that "from today, you
will be renewed and formed anew and made alive
again."[388] He initiates her into her new religion through
ritual actions that include the bread of life, the cup of
immortality, and the ointment of incorruptibility which
Joseph had mentioned previously. Thus converted and
initiated, Aseneth prepares for marriage to Joseph.

Although the ritual system and mystical outlook of
Joseph and Aseneth cannot be taken as representative of
all forms of Judaism in Late Antiquity, it offers vivid
evidence in at least one form of Judaism for an
understanding of conversion as a conscious decision to
abandon a former way of life. It involves a complete
reorientation of the soul of the convert and the entrance
into a new form of ritual practice if not into a specific
social community. The conversion to Judaism portrayed
in *Joseph and Aseneth*, along with the conversions of
Lucian and Justin, gives specific support to Nock's claim
that Judaism, Christianity, and certain forms of philosophy in the ancient world demanded a thorough conversion, rather than mere adhesion, of their participants. It
remains to examine Nock's claim that such conversion
was not required of the participants in the worship of
other deities.

The case that poses particular problems for Nock's
distinction is the account of the religious experience of
the narrator Lucius in the eleventh book of Apuleius'

ancient novel, *Metamorphoses* or *The Golden Ass*. Nock notes that "the external facts [of the narrative] are of course trustworthy";[389] they may even be autobiographical.[390] *The Golden Ass* recounts the amazing, and often ribald, adventures of its hero Lucius, primarily after an initial fascination with the practice of magic has the unintended and thoroughly unfortunate consequence of transforming him, literally, into an ass. Like the individual in "Amazing Grace" and like many other converts, Lucius has seen more than his share of "toils, troubles, and snares"[391] by the time that he finds himself exhausted on a beach at Cenchreae, a port of ancient Corinth. After a brief sleep, Lucius, still in the form of an ass, awakes to see a full moon; then:

> feeling that Fate was now satiated with my endless miseries and at last licensed a hope of salvation, I determined to implore the august image of the risen Goddess.[392]

Lucius' plea to the "Queen of Heaven" brings a quick and startling reply from the goddess who discloses her "true name, Queen Isis:"

> Behold, I am come to you in your calamity. I am come with solace and aid. Away then with tears. Cease to moan. Send sorrow packing. Soon through my providence shall the sun of your salvation arise.[393]

Isis instructs Lucius that at her festival on the next day he will be able to find and eat the roses which will serve as the antidote to reverse his magical transformation. Her graciousness is not without its requirements, however. As she tells Lucius:

> Only remember, and keep the remembrance fast in your heart's deep core, that all the remaining days of your life must be dedicated to me, and that nothing can release you from this service but death. . . .

> More, if you are found to merit my love by your dedicated obedience, religious devotion, and constant chastity, you will discover that it is within my power to prolong your life beyond the limits set to it by Fate. [394]

Lucius the ass eats the roses the next day and resumes his human shape. The crowd of onlookers marvels at the power of the goddess and suspects that "it is as though he had been set apart from the moment of his second birth for the ministry of heaven."[395] Lucius, instructed by a vision, proceeds to be initiated into the mysteries of Isis at Corinth; he subsequently is initiated into the mysteries of Osiris, and the mysteries of Isis in Rome, becoming a member of the professional priesthood at Isis' Roman temple.

Nock treats Lucius' case as an evident exception:

> Our survey of paganism has given us little reason to expect that the adhesion of any individual to a cult would involve any marked spiritual reorientation, any recoil from his moral and religious past, any idea of starting a new life.[396]

Lucius' experience represents for Nock "the high-water mark of the piety which grew out of the mystery religions."[397] If Lucius fits Nock's definition of conversion, as he obviously does, Nock does not see him as representative of the throng of worshippers of Isis that looked on in amazement as Lucius ate the roses and regained his human shape. Nock argues that Christianity, Judaism, and philosophy demanded conversion of all who would enter; the other Greco-Roman cults demanded no such thing. The intensity of Lucius' religious experience, and its impact on the rest of his life, is an aberration, not the typical case.

Nock's understanding of conversion has to be modified in the case of Lucius partially because Nock has inherited from James the focus on extraordinary individuals. The distinction between prophetic religions, which demand conversion, and traditional religions, which require only adhesion, weakens when it is brought to bear on Lucius. In its intensity, comprehensiveness, and effects, Lucius' transformation back into a human being and his initiation into the mysteries of Isis fits Nock's definition of a conversion. If the reported *experience*, not the religion, is to be explained, conversion is the appropriate explanatory category.

When Nock moves from the explanation of individual experience, for which James' theoretical perspective is so well suited, to the explanation of the broader historical impact of such individual experience, his fundamental distinctions begin to weaken. Nock's juxtaposition of psychological and historical questions, signaled in his early reference to "the mind of the time," pulls his argument in two different ways. The distinction between religions that demand conversion and religions that require only adhesion collapses when Nock turns to the religious experiences of extraordinary individuals. Jews and Christians, philosophers and priests of Isis alike seem to have experienced conversion. It is not the experience of Lucius that would allow Nock to distinguish the worship of Isis from Christianity, but the experience of those in the faceless crowd who marvelled at his transformation. Conversion was neither required nor typical of them, Nock argues. But Nock is pulled, by his Jamesian focus, away from a thorough consideration of the differences between the crowds of Isis-worshippers and the crowds of Christians. Time and again he leaves behind the crowd to return to the exaggerated cases of a few extraordinary examples, such as Lucius, Justin, and Augustine.

MacMullen's Theory of Conversion

Ramsay MacMullen, in *Christianizing the Roman Empire*, has also noticed the tension between psychological and historical interests in Nock's study of conversion. MacMullen argues that Nock has chosen "a focus for his discussion that is, if not theology, at least not history."[398] MacMullen locates the problem in "the fundamental assumption that religious belief does not deserve the name unless it is intense and consuming."[399] Familiarity with James' theory of religion in *The Varieties* makes it clear where Nock could have come by such an assumption. In terms of the analysis I have developed in earlier chapters, it is easy to see why Nock's concern appears to MacMullen to be theology. James' theory of religion, which is implicit in Nock's view of conversion, leads Nock to focus on extraordinary personal experience as it is recorded, for example, in Apuleius' *Golden Ass*, Justin's retelling of his own experience in the *Dialogue with Trypho*, and Augustine's *Confessions*. Contrary to James' expectations, however, such texts contain not only reports of religious experience, but also the explanations of that experience proposed by the subjects themselves. Those explanations typically attribute the experience in question to divine intervention, be it the action of Queen Isis or the Christian Holy Spirit. As such, then, converts' explanations are theological. As a result, Nock's Jamesian theory leads him directly to the study of theology, at least in its primary form of comments about divine activity by converts themselves. I have tried to suggest that such a focus ends up pulling Nock away from the task of explaining the historical expansion of Christianity. MacMullen finds it hopelessly inadequate to that task since it ignores "the overwhelming bulk of the Christian population."[400]

MacMullen takes an approach to the study of conversion that is poles apart from James' concentration on "the feelings, acts, and experiences of individual men in their solitude." As I will later discuss in more detail, his approach more closely resembles Robin Horton's explanation of the expansion of Christianity and Islam in sub-Saharan Africa. From the beginning, MacMullen clearly draws the lines of his inquiry. His subject "is the growth of the church as seen from the outside, and the period is the one that saw the church become dominant, and Europe Christian."[401] Furthermore, as he bluntly puts it, his "object is history. It might be, but it isn't, theology."[402] Like Nock, MacMullen wants to assess the historical significance of the rise of Christianity; he is, however, much less influenced by a Jamesian focus on "individual men in their solitude." MacMullen asserts that "it would be hard to picture the necessary scale of conversion if we limited ourselves to contexts and modes of persuasion that concerned only single individuals talking to each other."[403] In addition, a focus on autobiographical accounts of conversion by Christian intellectuals like Justin or Augustine cannot significantly inform an answer to the historical question MacMullen poses. Such figures

> belong to a particular type, "in every way very religious" (as one such person, a non-Christian, is described in a certain story). More than that, they represented a very high degree of cultivation. They had read whole libraries; some were even professional intellectuals making their living out of their extended studies. By two separate qualifications, then, these individuals stood apart from their world, a number almost too small to measure.[404]

Numbers are what MacMullen needs to explain the "Christianization" of the Roman empire. Historical significance "indicates the degree to which many people, not just a few, are made to live their lives differently in respects that much engage their thoughts, not in respects they do not think about very carefully."[405] Even if, for example, Justin's explanation of his own conversion to

Christianity as a conversion to philosophy is indicative of a broader process in which Christianity sought and eventually achieved a measure of philosophical and intellectual respectability, an historical explanation must be able to demonstrate how such a change occurred and how widely its effects were felt. If its impact was restricted to the small intellectual class in ancient society, it might not be considered one of the primary factors in the expansion of Christianity. As MacMullen claims, "Significance must be compounded of both 'many' and 'much' in a sort of multiplicand of the two elements."[406]

Despite their common interest in explaining the rise of Christianity, MacMullen puts the question differently than Nock and accordingly looks to different sources for his evidence. A single example can serve as the touchstone for his approach. In his *History of the Monks of Syria*, written around 444, the Christian bishop Theodoret of Cyrus records a tumultuous scene of conversion. In a vivid display of religious virtuosity that would certainly have captured James' eye, a fifth-century Christian named Symeon undertook to spend a good portion of his life standing on a pillar in the desert, some forty miles east of Antioch in Syria. Symeon's self-mortification, like that of other monks at the time, drew a crowd, many of whom, apparently, were moved to embrace his God. Theodoret describes one such incident:

> [Even the bedouins] in many thousands, enslaved to the darkness of impiety, were enlightened by the station upon the pillar. . . . They arrived in companies, 200 in one, 300 in another, occasionally a thousand. They renounced with their shouts their traditional errors; they broke up their venerated idols in the presence of that great light; and they foreswore the ecstatic rites of Aphrodite, the demon whose service they had long accepted. They enjoyed divine religious initiation and received their law instead spoken by that holy tongue (of Symeon). Bidding farewell to ancestral customs, they renounced also the diet of the wild ass or the camel. And I myself was witness to these things and heard them, as they renounced their ancestral piety and submitted to evangelic instruction.[407]

That eyewitness report of a mass conversion assumes paradigmatic importance for MacMullen. In the virtually spontaneous response of large crowds to such demonstrations of divine power he finds the key to an explanation of the growth of the Christian movement. MacMullen acknowledges that one might rightly question whether the bedouins in Theodoret's account had actually converted. He argues, however, that such questions may rely on an implicit assumption, such as the one he finds in Nock, that "religious belief does not deserve the name unless it is intense and consuming." In opposition, MacMullen contends that the historian "must be ready to recognize and to treat as religious history an almost unmanageably broad range of psychological phenomena, of which the most historically significant need not have been at all intense or complicated intellectually."[408] From that perspective conversion to Christianity can be defined as "that change of belief by which a person accepted the reality and supreme power of God and determined to obey Him."[409] That acceptance might be based on sophisticated theological or philosophical reasoning, but it could also be based on an immediate impression that the God of the Christians had concretely demonstrated his power. Such an apparently spontaneous and unreasoned conversion occurs in the apocryphal *Acts of John* when people in a crowd observe a miracle and declare: "[There is but] one god, [the god] of John. . . . We are converted, now that we have seen thy marvelous works! Have mercy upon us, O God, according to thy will, and save us from our great error."[410]

Only such mass conversions can offer a glimpse of the vast numerical increase of Christians in the ancient world. If every Christian convert had followed the slow, tortuous path of a Justin or Augustine, MacMullen suggests, Christianity could never have reached the numerical significance that it did. MacMullen explicitly rejects any attempts to sift through the evidence in an attempt to separate "true" conversions from false ones; to do so is to import a theological distinction into an historical argument. He contends that "it would be arbitrary to insist on a stricter definition of 'Christian' than did the church itself."[411] Accordingly, since Theodoret describes the throngs of bedouins as converts to Christianity, it is appropriate for the historian to do so. If the people who witness the apostle's miracle in the *Acts of John* declare themselves to be converts, then their testimony must be accepted.

In the analytical terms that I have used, MacMullen emphasizes accepting converts' own explanations of their experience. As he writes in a footnote, "my own focus is on conversion, arising from what people thought; so, if *they* believed the things they saw to be miraculous, that is enough for me."[412] Though he never develops such statements into an explicit theoretical position, and though he remains very suspicious of "anthropologizing" explanations, MacMullen's position has on the surface at least a few points in common with Horton's intellectualist explanation of African conversion. Like Horton, MacMullen is loath to disregard the explicit content of statements which express belief in the supernatural or miraculous. Initially, at least, they must be taken to mean what they say. As a result, the historian must be prepared to admit that very many people became Christians because they recognized the superior power of the Christian God. That does not necessarily mean that Theodoret's bedouins, for example, "returned to the desert without returning to their desert ways." MacMullen cannot imagine that, "in renouncing their little household icons, they also renounced the pillaging of their enemies and the avenging of their own dead."[413] Conversion for them did not mean a total transformation of the way they lived. If conversion were so narrowly defined, then they did not really enter the Christian church. But that would be to deny what Theodoret presents as their own explicit understanding of their experience. *They* thought that they had entered the church, and that for MacMullen (as it would for be Horton) is what matters. For MacMullen, the story of the growth of Christianity before Constantine is the story of conversions wrought by the miraculous demonstration of God's power. After the emperor's conversion in 312, the Christian church acquires a powerful patron and conversion can plausibly be attributed to a variety of new motives, though as Theodoret's account from 444 indicates miracles continued to provoke conversions.

MacMullen offers a clearer definition of the historical question than does Nock. It might be argued that he ignores other crucial factors in the long-term success of Christianity, but in many ways that would have to be an argument from silence, a silence populated with any number of unverifiable hypotheses. His insistence on taking the evidence of the texts at face value might be considered intentionally naive, but Horton has demonstrated the potential theoretical and explanatory power in such a view. MacMullen, at least, has successfully avoided the contradictory pulls of Nock's twin interests in questions of individual psychology and historical change by refusing to collapse one into the other.

If MacMullen's position can be identified as a sort of "common sense intellectualism," however, it is unfortunate that he seems not to know the work of Horton. As I have shown in the previous chapter Horton has pushed beyond the relatively simple yield of the intellectualist approach—that analysis should begin with people's explicit explanations of their own behavior—to a rich explanation of the role of African conversion to Christianity and Islam in the broader historical, social, and cultural processes of modernization. Horton's approach suggests that a full intellectualist explanation of conversion to Christianity in Late Antiquity would attempt to set it more fully within the relevant complex of historical, cultural, and social changes. In some ways MacMullen's account of conversion to Christianity after Constantine's conversion in 312 begins that task, but much remains to be done in both the earlier and later periods. MacMullen has not exhausted the topic of the significance of conversion to Christianity for the transformation of the ancient world.

Conclusions

With Horton and MacMullen the study of conversion is set into its broadest context. In their approaches the intimate personal details that were so important for William James, and consequently for so many other interpreters of religious conversion, recede into the background. For them, the personal is much more idiosyncratic than indicative. The feelings, acts, and experiences of extraordinary individuals in their solitude are not necessarily the stuff of historical change. With MacMullen and Horton, attention is directed to the great, undifferentiated mass of believers, to those whose experience James found to be inaccessible, unrecoverable, and uninteresting. MacMullen, of course, would disagree with James. What is interesting is all in the eye of the observer. James asked a certain type of question, based on certain explicit assumptions. It is not, however, the only type of question that can be asked.

Conversion, in fact, proves to be a rather malleable phenomenon. It can yield interesting information to psychologists, theologians, sociologists, anthropologists, and historians alike. In defining the phenomenon, each observer is actually defining what is of particular interest about it, not what it is in itself. As Jonathan Z. Smith has persuasively argued, the observer, in effect, *creates* the object of study, be it the specific phenomenon of conversion or the broader category of religion. In either instance, the object of study "is created for the scholar's analytic purposes by his imaginative acts of comparison and generalization."[414]

I have argued that the reciprocal movement between a general theory of religion and the specific analysis of conversion can be identified in works as diverse as James' *The Varieties of Religious Experience*, Barth's *Church Dogmatics*, Lofland and Stark's "Becoming a World Saver," Horton's series of articles on African conversion, Nock's *Conversion*, and MacMullen's *Christianizing the Roman Empire*. When the observers focus specifically on conversion, their comments imply a general theory of religion. When they discuss religion in theoretical terms, those comments determine how they will describe, analyze, and explain conversion. In each case, the observers' commitments to particular explanatory theories determine what questions they will ask, what answers they will get, and what information they will accept as evidence.

The study of conversion, however, has not been marked solely by the creative free play of the scholarly imagination. Diverse as they might be, the examples considered up to this point have all been taken from the spheres of influence of the Western religious traditions of Judaism, Christianity, and Islam. As in so many other cases, the roots of the concept of conversion go back to Western, and Christian, antiquity. That in itself creates no problems if we adapt James' concern with fruits and not roots to the category of conversion.[415] Conversion has proved, so far, to be an interesting and instructive point of entry into the study of religions as diverse as Sun Myung Moon's Unification Church, the African independent Apostolic Church of John Maranke, and the Judaism represented by the romance of *Joseph and Aseneth*. But the absence of conversion from definitions of religion as diverse as those of Emile Durkheim, Clifford Geertz, and Paul Tillich should arouse the suspicion that conversion might not be an essential defining characteristic of religion. Further, it might not be a universal or even widespread characteristic. It would, of course, cause no great difficulties if conversion were to be a category of religious activity only within the general orbits of Judaism, Christianity, and Islam. One would have only to use the category with the appropriate constraints in mind. Before such constraints are accepted, however, it will be helpful to inquire whether the category can have even broader utility. I will address that issue, and others, in the concluding chapter.

Conclusion: Description, Analysis, and Interpretation of Religious Conversion

Taking Stock

In 1981 John Lofland and Norman Skonovd argued that the literature on conversion had become so rich and diverse that "a pause and provisional stock-taking"[416] was in order. This book has been such a stock-taking, though it has proceeded from a rather different set of assumptions. Throughout the book I have argued that implicit and explicit theoretical assumptions will decisively influence what the observer of religious conversion looks for. William James' definition of religion as the "feelings, acts, and experiences of individual men in their solitude" provides the classic case in point. Further, what the observer is looking *for* also directly influences what type of data will be looked *at*. Since, for example, Robin Horton was looking for an explanation of the continent-wide trend of conversion to Islam and Christianity in Africa, he looked at different data than would someone who was interested in the contours and meaning of the individual conversion experience. In a similar vein, I have suggested that Arthur Darby Nock's *Conversion* reveals the incommensurability of what he was looking for, an explanation of the rise of Christianity, and what he looked at, stories of individual Christian converts. Finally, what an observer looks for and what that observer looks at are the crucial determinants of what the observer will actually see. For example, James will see conversion as an individual experience and Lofland and Stark will see it as a social process, not because the data at which they are looking are somehow intrinsically different in themselves but because their theoretical assumptions and methodological procedures lead them to look at things in one way and not another. As I have consistently proposed, it should be possible, and instructive, to study any given instance of conversion, so long as the information is available, from a number of points of view. Stephen Bradley's autobiographical pamphlet, for example, clearly can be made by James to testify about his personal experience. In the hands of someone else, however, it could easily become a source of information about the social relationships and processes in which Bradley was enmeshed or about the theological convictions that shaped his own understanding of his conversion.

I am thus not willing to go along with Lofland and Skonovd in claiming that "the differences among conversion experiences which investigators are reporting with increasing frequency are not simply a matter of the 'theoretical goggles' worn by the researchers."[417] Seeing things through such theoretical goggles is not a simple matter. Such lenses can clarify through magnification or through intensifying the focus to isolate some things in the field of vision and to exclude others, but, when they have a certain tint, they can also color anything that comes within view with a definite hue. The burden of my argument has been that theoretical commitments play a crucial role in shaping how one defines and understands conversion. Observers can only see clearly by donning some sort of theoretical goggles, and such goggles have the enormous clarifying power of the strongest corrective lenses.

Lofland and Skonovd argue, however, that it is the experiences themselves, rather than the theoretical constructions of them, that differ. They claim that "such differences are inherent in the central or key features of conversions themselves."[418] With that assertion they raise the questions about the nature of religious experience and the observer's access to it that I considered in the first chapter. In that chapter I contrasted James' approach, which presumed ready and direct access to individual experience, with that of Proudfoot, which emphasizes instead that any report about personal experience, even first-hand reports like Bradley's pamphlet, will present experience that is "already informed and constituted by our conceptions and tacit theories about ourselves and our world."[419] I have argued that Proudfoot's analysis is much more compelling; it poses a stumbling block for Lofland and Skonovd as well.

Lofland and Skonovd would distinguish three separate levels of social reality. They dub the first "raw reality." That level accords with James' characterization of experience as "all that sort of thing immediately and privately felt."[420] The second level is that of conversion accounts, the stories that people tell about their own conversions. In addition, "the efforts of analysts may be thought of, indeed, as a third level of social reality—one that tries to keep pace, often unsuccessfully, with the ever-changing character of the first two levels."[421] In theoretical terms, Lofland and Skonovd's crucial assertion is that "it is probable that [conversion accounts] reflect 'raw reality'."[422] In their perception, the transparency of such accounts allows them to see through them to the underlying social reality and thus to make forms of *experience* their primary subject. Lofland and Skonovd proceed to classify conversion experiences according to six motifs: intellectual, mystical, experimental, affectional, revivalist, and coercive, and five variables in the intellectual, physical, and emotional realms: degree of social pressure, temporal duration, level of affective arousal, affective content, and belief-participation sequence.[423] Their article gives a clear exposition of each type of conversion.

Lofland and Skonovd's classification of the types of conversion experience is certainly fuller and more complex than James' simple division into conversion by self-surrender and volitional conversion, but it betrays a similar confidence about the accessibility of personal experience, as such, to the observer. In their presentation, conversion accounts primarily "reflect" raw reality. Although they concede that such raw realty is "ambiguously and imperfectly available to us," they still assert that conversion accounts are "structured by the first level and by any particular paradigm found useful to the convert to interpret the former."[424] Experience determines ("structures," "is reflected in") conversion accounts. While Lofland and Skonovd acknowledge the imprecise nature of the information that conversion accounts supply about experience and the possible influence of paradigms of understanding on such accounts, they still emphasize that the raw reality of a conversion experience exercises a primary influence on any accounts of it. In the first chapter I argued that Proudfoot provides a persuasive alternative to such a view. Concerning the concepts, commitments, and expectations which someone brings to any new experience, he argues that "beliefs and attitudes are formative of, rather than consequent upon, the experience. They define in advance what experiences are possible."[425] Proudfoot's position would lead to at least a partial reversal of the relationship between experience and the complex pattern of concepts, commitments, and expectations that an individual brings to any experience. To use Lofland and Skonovd's terms, such prior beliefs and attitudes structure experience and are reflected in it.

As I take stock, then, of the contemporary study of religious conversion, I part company with Lofland and Skonovd on two important issues. First, I find that theoretical commitments decisively influence what an observer looks for, looks at, and sees. One's "theoretical goggles" are of crucial importance. Second, I choose to emphasize more strongly the profound shaping influence that both prior and newly acquired beliefs and commitments have upon individuals' understanding and presentation of their own experience. Several consequences follow from that position. In agreement with Proudfoot I assert that individuals can only experience what they can conceive. Stephen Bradley, for example, did not attribute the physical symptoms that accompanied his conversion to the activity of Zeus or Krishna. He could not conceive of such a possibility. Both his prior experience (his first "conversion" at age fourteen) and his immediate circumstances (attendance at a revival meeting), however, made it quite possible for him to interpret his physical symptoms as the activity of the Christian Holy Spirit. In Proudfoot's terms, they defined in advance what experiences were possible for Bradley.

Conversion accounts, moreover, are not only subject to the shaping influence of prior experience and immediate circumstances. Since any account is to some extent retrospective, the presentation of experience (and therefore the "experience" itself) can change as the situation of the convert changes. Jules-Rosette notes that in her case "part of the dramatic impact of the conversion experience emerged through examining it and constructing it in retrospect."[426] As she changed her understanding of her experience also changed. Since there is, however, no independent attestation of her experience, it is proper to claim that as Jules-Rosette's understanding of her experiences changes so does the experience itself.

To the extent that my assertion is accurate Lofland and Skonovd's position that the raw reality of experience "structures" conversion accounts and that those accounts, in turn, "reflect," however ambiguously and imperfectly, raw reality, is called into question. In "Becoming a World-Saver Revisited" Lofland urged that attention be given to "how people go about converting themselves."[427] I suggest that one dimension of that process concerns how they continually adjust their accounts of conversion to reflect their current situations, commitments, and beliefs. In effect, as Jules-Rosette shows, converts are continually "converting their conversions" to bring them into closer harmony with their current circumstances. In that view "experience," rather than appearing as something fixed and determinative, becomes something more fluid and malleable; conversion accounts, rather than reflections of "raw reality," become constructions of it. If such is the case, the role of the observer changes too. Unlike Lofland and Skonovd, I choose to view conversion accounts as *first order explanations* of conversion. Like any explanations, they are shaped in important ways by the concrete situation of the person doing the explaining, and, as that situation changes, so also will the explanation.

In accordance with that position, I have tried throughout this book to re-orient the discussion of conversion away from the reconstruction of experience and toward the discussion of explanations. In many ways that attempt stems from my intention to conceive of religion as something that happens in society, rather than solely within the individual. I choose to conceive of religion as something that is primarily public and social, rather than private and individual. In so doing, I display a marked affinity for explanations of religion that George Lindbeck has called "cultural-linguistic" rather than "experiential-expressivist."[428] Lindbeck attributes the following positions to the experiential-expressivist model of religion

(1) Different religions are diverse expressions or objectifications of a common core experience. It is this experience which identifies them as religions.
(2) The experience, while conscious, may be unknown on the level of self-conscious reflection. (3) It is present in all human beings. (4) In most religions, the experience is the source and norm of objectifications: it is by reference to the experience that their adequacy or lack of adequacy is to be judged.[429]

In contrast, the cultural-linguistic model of religion views it "as a kind of cultural and/or linguistic framework or medium that shapes the entirety of life and thought."[430] Thus,

> it is similar to an idiom that makes possible the description of realities, the formulation of beliefs, and the experiencing of inner attitudes, feelings, and sentiments. Like a culture or language, it is a communal phenomenon that shapes the subjectivities of individuals rather than being primarily a manifestation of those objectivities. It comprises a vocabulary of discursive and nondiscursive symbols together with a distinctive logic or grammar in terms of which this vocabulary can be meaningfully deployed.[431]

Lindbeck's observation that religions shape individual subjectivities rather than manifesting them states in broader form my argument against Lofland and Skonovd.

Converts and external observers share the desire to account for conversion, to explain it in accessible terms. Though they have different relationships to the experience in question and different conceptions of the audience for the explanation, both share the desire to make sense of the apparent change. To do so, they draw upon a fund of beliefs and concepts that is the common property of the communities to which they belong. In each case, prior commitments and experiences, along with current circumstances, define in advance the types of explanation that will be intelligible and acceptable. Conversion stories use the vocabulary of the convert's new community to give shape and meaning to the perceived personal transformation. As Lindbeck phrases it in his description of the cultural-linguistic model of religion, that vocabulary *makes possible* the description of the convert's experience.

Where Lofland and Skonovd, and many others, are concerned with levels of reality and the recovery of experience, I have been concerned with types of explanation and the uncovering of theoretical perspectives. I have distinguished between *primary or first order* explanations, those offered by converts themselves, and *secondary or second order* explanations, those offered by external observers. As the case of Benetta Jules-Rosette illustrates, that distinction is not the same as the one between convert and scholar. I have further stressed that both primary and secondary explanations of conversion can take a variety of forms. As far as I can determine, there is no necessary connection between a claimed experience and a particular explanation of it. Stephen Bradley, for example, chose to explain his conversion in a certain way. As Proudfoot has clearly shown, however, neither Bradley's nor James' are the only possible explanations of that conversion. Similarly, within the ranks of college-age converts to the Unification Church significant differences of emphasis emerge in the primary explanations of conversion. While Christopher Edwards tends to see himself as the passive dupe of cunning recruiters, Barbara Underwood tends to see herself as an active seeker of truth and a loving community. Secondary explanations of conversion to the Unification Church display an even wider range. From the scenario of demonological possession that lies at the heart of deprogramming's rationale, through the milder therapeutic model of "exit counseling" of various sorts, to the "love-bombing" on behalf of the Heavenly Kingdom practiced by happy California "Moonies", the act of conversion to the Unification Church is construed in wildly diverse fashions. A similar diversity marks the views in scholarly and popular publications, though the former display a fondness for social-psychological explanations along the lines suggested by Lofland and Stark and the latter rarely depart from a crass sensationalism.

In each chapter I have shown that explanations of conversion, either primary or secondary, express the fundamental interests of the person doing the explaining. James' interest in religion as an individual phenomenon decisively shapes his treatment of conversion; Barth's consideration of conversion within the *Church Dogmatics* depends upon his theological interests; sociologists like Lofland and Stark will ask questions about conversion that psychologists, philosophers, and theologians most likely will not; anthropologists with a historical bent, like Horton, will in turn ask still a different set of questions. In each instance the questions asked are determined by a certain set of interests and assumptions, and the questions themselves define in advance what types of answers are possible.

Lofland and Skonovd remark that James, and other scholars writing about conversion at the beginning of this century, focused on the mystical type of conversion. They suggest that "the reason for this might have been its more widespread incidence in late nineteenth and early twentieth century America."[432] They observe further that "it seems to have attracted less interest among converts and scholars (who simply follow converts) in the middle third of the twentieth century save as a minor topic within psychoanalytical analysis."[433] My understanding of matters leads me to a different explanation. I would grant pride of place to James' explicit theoretical program; he focused on mystical conversions because he was intensely interested in instances of "direct personal communion with the divine."[434] It was that interest, explicitly stated and defended in the opening chapters of *The Varieties*, that led James to chose for discussion the examples that he did. I would not want at all to deny any influence of James' historical context on his theoretical position, but, nonetheless, his theoretical position was consciously and carefully formulated to guide his inquiries. *The Varieties* does not simply reflect the time in which it was written, and James ranges far afield from the United States in the late nineteenth century for his examples.

Moreover, it is not at all clear that scholars "simply follow converts." It is sufficient to read both James and Proudfoot on Stephen Bradley to be disabused of that notion. Scholars look for converts for particular reasons, because they want to make some specific points. Depending upon which points they wish to make, they will look at different types of information. Given their interests and assumptions, they will see different things. Nock and MacMullen, for example, value the testimony of Augustine's *Confessions* in very different ways. They do not "simply follow the convert." Nock, as I have shown, follows James, and follows him so faithfully that he fails to achieve his objective. MacMullen follows a different lead and consequently devalues the testimony of individual intellectuals like Augustine in favor of evidence about the conversion of large numbers of people. It is impossible simply to follow the converts because their testimonies will take on different meanings in different interpretive contexts. Just as singing "Amazing Grace" at a country-and-western bar means something rather different from singing it at a worship service, so will the meaning of a conversion account vary from one context to the next. I contend that the crucial determinant of such differences is to be found in the explanatory interests and assumptions of the observer, rather than in the historical context or the nature of the experience itself. To be sure, any theory must take adequate account of the data it considers. I propose, however, that the theory plays the essential role of defining what will be accepted as evidence in the first place. One need only return to James' sweeping exclusion of ritual, theology, and community life for confirmation of that proposal.[435]

James, in fact, is exemplary in his willingness to describe fully his theoretical assumptions and interests and to carry them through his description, analysis, and interpretation of conversion. It is possible to agree or disagree with James on an informed basis because he describes so clearly his goals and the means by which he will attain them. Not all observers are so forthcoming. I turn now to a negative example, in which, because no questions are clearly asked, no answers are given.

No Questions, No Answers

In his general discussion of religions of conversion and religions of adhesion Nock mentions "Gotama the Buddha" as an example of the prophet who has the ability "to express and to appear to meet the half-formed prayers of some at least of his contemporaries."[436] If the Buddha fits the description of a prophet, then Buddhism would be a prophetic religion, and, by Nock's own description, would demand conversion. Nock, unfortunately, does not pursue his suggestion. He is far from alone, however, in using "conversion" to describe the experience of the Buddha and his earliest disciples.[437] Because the descriptions of the Buddha's enlightenment and the decisions of his first disciples are described as self-evidently conversions, it should prove worthwhile to inquire further about what scholars may have meant by using such a term. What questions were they asking that the category of conversion seemed to help them arrive at convincing answers?

Though the historical Buddha lived from 567 to 483 B.C.E., the first full biographies were not composed until the fifth century C.E.[438] A very complex biographical tradition took shape in the intervening 900 years. Despite careful attempts to sift that evidence for nuggets of historical fact, in the view of one recent commentator, "it is impossible to reconstruct anything like a complete narrative which can claim historical authenticity."[439] The historical Buddha is certainly no more accessible than the historical Jesus; both lie covered under layers of tradition which have been molded and reshaped by successive generations of the faithful in order to suit their own religious needs, not the needs of modern scholars.

The inaccessibility of the historical Buddha raises questions about Nock's brief allusion to his prophetic activity and also about any description of his enlightenment as a conversion. As I showed in the previous chapter, Nock adopted with little alteration both James' definition of conversion and the theory of religion that goes with it. That decision led him to look for well-developed first-hand accounts of religious experiences in Late Antiquity. He saw, for example, in Apuleius' *Golden Ass* a "trustworthy" account of personal religious experience.[440] Given the state of the biographical tradition about the Buddha, however, it is difficult to see how a Jamesian approach could yield any significant results. James, with his professed concern for the original experiences of religious geniuses and his reliance on first-hand accounts of such experiences, would not be able to find his quarry in the luxuriant growth of the biographical traditions about the Buddha.[441] Far from affording direct access to the Buddha's consciousness and immediate experience, the texts testify to the ways in which the life of the Buddha was embellished and adapted by successive generations of interpreters in the various schools of Buddhist thought that developed after the Buddha's demise. In Lindbeck's terms, they provide abundant information about the religious vocabulary of different phases and schools of Buddhism, but much less about the experiences of the historical Buddha. If Nock meant to suggest that the observer could find in the life of the Buddha material that would provide significant and extensive direct testimony about the feelings, acts, and experiences of that historical individual, modern scholarship decisively rules out that possibility.

If for analytical purposes the Buddha can not be considered an ancient Indian counterpart of Stephen Bradley, because his personal feelings, acts, and experiences are likely to remain forever hidden from view, the "particularly serious interest which the early compilers showed in the [Buddha's] Enlightenment and the events immediately preceding and following it"[442] still needs to be examined. As I have noted, scholars have tended to invoke the category of conversion as a description, and implicitly an analysis and interpretation, of those events. While their use of the term is clear, their intentions are much less so. Since it is not clear what kinds of questions the category of conversion might have helped them ask, it is much less clear what answers they produced and precisely what those answers might mean.

Consider, for example, Edward J. Thomas' *The Life of Buddha as Legend and History*. At several points in his summary and analysis of the Buddha's "great renunciation" of wealth and pleasure Thomas describes the change that took place as a conversion.[443] The impetus for that description is perhaps clarified by a comparison that Thomas draws between a passage about the birth of the Buddha and a passage in the gospel according to Luke. Thomas claims only that the Lukan passage provides a parallel, but it seems clear that he intends the parallel somehow to be instructive. By bringing the Buddha into comparison with Jesus, Thomas implicitly suggests that the course of the Buddha's life, and perhaps the course of Buddhism as well, can be understood in analogy with Jesus and Christianity. Analytical categories that prove fruitful in one case are assumed to be fruitful in the other. Aside from the fact that comparability is presumed rather than demonstrated, it is not at all clear what Thomas, and the others who have used the term, mean by "conversion."

Unlike Nock, Thomas gives no indication of the source of his analytical category. For him, the term "conversion" has a self-evident clarity; he also uses it to describe the experience of the first five followers of the Buddha.[444] As I have shown, however, conversion, like any other analytical category, is highly malleable. In the hands of William James it acquires a clarity and definition quite distinct from those it has for Karl Barth. For Lofland and Stark, it delimits a phenomenon whose scope and extent are much different than they are for James or Barth. In each case, how conversion is described is intimately linked to how it will be analyzed and interpreted. Robin Horton certainly describes, analyzes, and interprets conversion in Africa much differently than would James, Barth, or Lofland and Stark. Thus, to describe the Buddha's experience as a conversion only begs a set of related questions. Unfortunately, those questions have not been taken up by Thomas and others who have apparently considered the meaning of the description to be self-evidently clear.

As I indicated earlier, it seems virtually impossible to take the surviving accounts of the Buddha's enlightenment as first-hand testimonies of personal experience. There is nothing in the biographical tradition about the

Buddha that compares to the direct testimony of Stephen Bradley's conversion account, let alone Augustine's *Confessions*. The distance between the individual feelings, acts, and experiences of the concrete, historical individual who became the Buddha and the embellishments of the biographical tradition can not be easily bridged. While a certain type of experience may lie at the foundation of the biographical tradition, it cannot be described in detail with any certainty. Ironically, the biographical tradition about the Buddha could more accurately be described with the phrases that James uses to describe the "ordinary religious believer."

> His religion has been made for him by others, communicated to him by tradition, determined to fixed forms by imitation, and retained by habit.[445]

As the work of generations of representatives from various Buddhist schools, the biographical tradition about the Buddha certainly does contain accounts of religious experiences that were "made for him by others;" successive layers of tradition have enlarged the account of his life to include incidents which speak not of the experiences of the Buddha but of the concerns of Buddhists. The inappropriateness of the James/Nock approach to the data does not mean, however, that the category of conversion itself is useless. It must, however, be conceived in a different manner if it is to be useful.

That the biographical tradition speaks more of the concerns of Buddhists than of the experiences of the Buddha suggests, for example, that it could be a rich source of Buddhist thinking about the form and meaning of the Buddha's enlightenment. Just as Karl Barth, reflecting on examples of Christian conversion, developed a normative view of "true conversion," so also do Buddhist scholars develop normative views of "true enlightenment." One early indication of that process can be seen in the ways that the stories in several texts of the "conversions" of the earliest disciples are modelled on the enlightenment of the Buddha.[446] If it is true that for Barth conversion becomes a shorthand experession for the Christian life, then enlightenment could become a shorthand experession for the Buddhist life.

The distance of the biographical tradition from the experience of the historical Buddha would also complicate the type of analysis that Lofland and Stark favor. They would be unable to observe or to reconstruct with any precision the social situation of the Buddha in its ancient Indian context. Yet since the texts concerning the conversions of the earliest disciples develop extensive parallels between their experiences and those of the Buddha, it might be possible to disengage from the texts an early idealized model of the Buddhist conversion process.

In many ways, Horton's (and to some extent MacMullen's) questions might be most profitably asked of the material. Horton would seek the broader social, cultural, and historical factors that gave further impetus to conversion to Buddhism as it developed in India and then moved into other areas of Asia. Horton's disinclination to depend upon the testimony of isolated individuals would serve him well in this case. Conjecture about how various scholars might treat the question of conversion to Buddhism, however, only underlines the fact that those who have already addressed the topic have formed no clear agenda. Only with difficulty is it possible to formulate what sorts of questions they may have been asking and what types of answers they expected to get.

Though this brief consideration of conversion to Buddhism serves mainly as a negative example, an instance of how not to study conversion, it has raised some issues that might be worth further study. Nock's initial impulse, to construct a typology of religions and to isolate those types in which conversion was likely to occur, was not really carried through. He developed not a typology but a rough-and-ready distinction between conversion and adhesion. Nonetheless, he pointed the way to a careful, cross-cultural comparison that has yet to be pursued. Certainly, random references to the conversion of the Buddha or his early disciples do not take up that task in any well-informed and systematic way. It remains to be seen whether the category of conversion can have any analytical usefulness beyond the orbits of Judaism, Christianity, and Islam. What is certain is that the investigator's questions will have to be framed much more carefully than they have been so far. Casual use of the term and random identification of parallels in themselves disclose nothing.

Conclusions

In my opening discussion of "Amazing Grace" I argued that the study of religion cannot rest content with accepting the claim of the hymn. The study of religion seeks not to marvel, to claim that something is amazing, but to understand, to take something apart in order to see how it works. There are, however, many ways in which the tasks of description, analysis, and interpretation can proceed. The observer's own interests and assumptions are what give direction to the process of understanding. They lead the observer to choose something, rather than something else, as an object of study. They also lead the observer to treat that something in a certain way. As a result, the claims and arguments that an individual observer makes derive their particular character from the interests and assumptions that inform them.

Virtually all of the thinkers considered in this book set out to study something called "conversion." It has become patently apparent, however, that few, if any, of them agree on the definition of the subject they supposedly have in common. As it turns out, all of them have delimited the phenomenon of conversion in such a way as to suit their interests. What they were looking for or what they were trying to explain, be it an individual experience, a social process, the activity of God in the world, or a process of historical change, decisively influenced what they would look at. Once they determined what they would look at, what they saw came as no surprise.

Forming an understanding of religious conversion involves, explicitly or implicitly, developing a much broader sense of what religion is, how it functions in human life, and what its meaning might be. Because that is true, the study of conversion offers an interesting starting point for the study of religion. For example, William James' comments on conversion introduced the issue of how individual religious experience is to be understood, and Wayne Proudfoot's response to James provided a clear alternative. Karl Barth's analysis of conversion provided an example of a Christian theologian at work, attempting to bring clarity and coherence to the inherited tradition. John Lofland, Rodney Stark, and the other sociologists considered in chapter three brought to the fore questions about the interaction of individuals with their immediate social environment. Robin Horton, along with Arthur Darby Nock and Ramsay MacMullen, raised broad questions about the role of religion in significant historical change. In addition to those, and other, issues which have been raised, the testimonies of individual converts, from the well-known examples of Malcolm X and Augustine of

Hippo, through current and former Moonies and members of independent African Christian churches, to Justin, the early Christian teacher and martyr, and Lucius, the well-traveled hero of the *Golden Ass*, have consistently and vividly displayed the vitality and complexity of religion in individual lives. To form a sense of what religion is and how it works it is necessary to attend both to the immediate particularity of the evidence at hand and to the broader questions of how that evidence might be understood. This book has attempted to do both.

Notes

¹Jonathan Z. Smith, *To Take Place* (Chicago: University of Chicago Press, 1987) p. xi.

²The full text of "Amazing Grace," by John Newton, can be easily found in Protestant hymnals.

³Jacob Neusner, in many of his works, has cogently and consistently described the tasks of the study of religion as description, analysis, and explanation. See particularly his *Ancient Judaism and Modern Category Formation* (Lanham, MD: University Press of America, 1986). I have learned much about the academic study of religion from Professor Neusner during a summer institute and a summer seminar sponsored by the National Endowment for the Humanities.

⁴Bennetta Jules-Rosette, *African Apostles: Ritual and Conversion in the church of John Maranke* (Ithaca: Cornell University Press, 1975) p. 69.

⁵(ps.-) Justin, *Discourse to the Greeks*, 5. For a translation of that text and the rest of Justin's works see Saint Justin Martyr. *Writings of Saint Justin Martyr*, Thomas B. Falls, trans., (New York: Christian Heritage, Inc., 1948; Fathers of the Church, vol. 6).

⁶Christopher Edwards, *Crazy for God* (Englewood Cliffs, NJ: Prentice-Hall, 1979) p. ix.

⁷William James, *The Varieties of Religious Experience* (New York: New American Library, 1958) p. 42.

⁸Emile Durkheim, *The Elementary Forms of the Religious Life*, Joseph W. Swain, trans. (New York: Free Press, 1915) p. 62.

⁹Clifford Geertz, "Religion as a Cultural System" in *The Interpretation of Cultures* (New York: Basic Books, 1973) pp. 87-125.

¹⁰Cf. Bernard Lonergan, "The Dimensions of Conversion" in Walter Conn, ed., *Conversion: Perspectives on Personal and Social Transformation* (New York: Alba House, 1978) pp. 15-21, esp. p. 18.

¹¹Cf. James, *The Varieties*, p. 24.

¹²For an investigation of how the theology of a group can shape converts' accounts of their experience see James A. Beckford, "Accounting for Conversion," *British Journal of Sociology* 29 (1978): 249-262; Brian Taylor, "Conversion and Cognition: An Area for Empirical Study in the Microsociology of Religious Knowledge," *Social Compass* 23 (1976): 5-22; and Taylor, "Recollection and Membership: Converts' Talk and the

Ratiocination of Commonality," *Sociology* 12 (1978): 316-324.

[13] Lewis R. Rambo, "Current Research on Religious Conversion," *Religious Studies Review* 8 (1982): 146-159.

[14] For Charles Colson, see his autobiographical *Born Again* (New York: Bantam Books, 1977); for Eldridge Cleaver see John A. Oliver, *Eldridge Cleaver: Reborn* (Plainfield, NJ: Logos International, 1977). For a critical review of the biblical background of the notion of being "born again" see Beverly Roberts Gaventa, *From Darkness to Light: Conversion in the New Testament* (Philadelphia: Fortress, 1986).

[15] James, *The Varieties* p. 157.

[16] Ibid., p. 162.

[17] Ibid., p. 186.

[18] Ibid., p. 346.

[19] As quoted in John J. Shea, *Religious Experiencing: William James and Eugene Gendlin* (Lanhan, MD: University Press of America, 1987) p. 9.

[20] James, *The Varieties*, p. 28, note (continued from p. 27).

[21] Ibid., p. 42.

[22] Ibid., p. 41.

[23] Ibid.

[24] Ibid., p. 42.

[25] Ibid., p. 24.

[26] Ibid., p. 24, my emphasis.

[27] Ibid., cf. p. 56.

[28] Ibid., p. 35.

[29] Ibid., p. 52.

[30] Ibid., p. 329.

[31] Ibid., cf. pp. 39, 40, 368.

[32] Cf. Rudolf Otto, *The Idea of the Holy*, John W. Harvey, trans. (Oxford: Oxford University Press, 1950, 2nd ed.).

[33] James, *The Varieties*, p. 73.

[34] Ibid.

[35] Ibid., p. 379.

[36] Ibid., p. 292.

[37] Ibid., cf. p. 208.

[38] Ibid., p. 42.

[39] Ibid., p. 40.

[40] Ibid., p. 34.

[41] Ibid., p. 22.

[42] Ibid., p. 137.

[43] Ibid., p. 371.

[44] Ibid., p. 143.

[45] Ibid., cf. p. 147.

[46] Ibid., p. 112.

[47] Ibid., p. 141.

[48] Ibid., p. 56.

[49] Ibid., p. 384.

[50] Ibid., p. 198.

[51] Ibid., p. 205.

[52] Ibid., p. 196.

[53] Wayne Proudfoot, *Religious Experience* (Berkeley: University of California Press, 1985), p. 43; cf. pp. 61, 66, 71.

[54] Ibid., p. 43.

[55] James, *The Varieties*, p. 157.

[56] Ibid.

[57] Proudfoot, *Religious Experience*, p. 104.

[58] Ibid., p. 107.

[59] Ibid.

[60] On James' life and career see Gerald E. Myers, *William James: His Life and Thought* (New Haven: Yale University Press, 1986) pp. 1-53.

[61] Proudfoot, *Religious Experience*, p. 114.

[62] Ibid., p. 121.

[63] James, *The Varieties*, p. 331.

[64] Ibid., p. 162.

[65] Malcolm X, with Alex Haley, *The Autobiography of Malcolm X* (New York: Ballantine Books, 1973), cf. p. 5.

[66] Cf. ibid., p. 16.

[67] Cf. ibid., p. 19.

[68] Ibid., pp. 36-37.

[69] Cf. James, *The Varieties*, pp. 172-173.

[70] Malcolm X, *Autobiography*, p. 14.

[71] Ibid.

[72] Ibid., p. 21.

[73] Proudfoot, *Religious Experience*, p. 121.

[74] Malcolm X, *Autobiography*, p. 150.

[75] Ibid., p. 155.

[76] Ibid. p. 156.

[77] Ibid.

[78] Proudfoot, *Religious Experience*, p. 112.

[79] Cf. James, *The Varieties*, pp. 169, 191.

[80] Proudfoot, *Religious Experience*. p. 61.

[81] Malcolm X, *Autobiography*, p. 161.

[82] Ibid.

[83] Ibid., p. 252.

[84] Cf. ibid., p. 2.

[85] Ibid., p. 174.

[86] Ibid., p. 183.

[87] Ibid., p. 163.

[88] Ibid., p. 164.

[89] Cf. ibid., p. 159.

[90] Cf. ibid., pp. 169, 197, 252.

[91] Ibid., p. 173.

[92] Cf. ibid., p. 208.

[93] Ibid., p. 330.

[94] Ibid., pp. 333-334.

[95] Ibid., p. 321.

[96] Ibid., p. 323.

[97] Ibid.

[98] Ibid., p. 340, his emphasis; cf. p. 170.

[99] Proudfoot, *Religious Experience*, p. 112.

[100] Cf. ibid., pp. 107, 108, 216.

[101] Cf. James, *The Varieties*, p. 158.

[102] Proudfoot, *Religious Experience*, p. 194.

[103] Ibid., p. 195.

[104] Cf. Malcolm X, *Autobiography*, pp. 24, 38, 149, 188, 211, 250.

[105] Ibid., p. 125.

[106] Cf. ibid., p. 200.

[107] For a vivid and thorough depiction of Augustine's life see Peter Brown, *Augustine of Hippo: A Biography* (Berkeley: University of California Press, 1967).

[108] Augustine, *Confessions*, III.4..

[109] Ibid., cf. III.6.

[110] Ibid., cf. IV.1; on Augustine's time among the Manichaeans see Brown, *Augustine of Hippo*, pp. 46-60.

[111] Cf. Augustine, *Confessions*, V.7, V.14.

[112] Cf. ibid., V.14.

[113] Cf. ibid., VII.9.

[114] Ibid., VIII.1-2.

[115] Ibid., VIII.7.

[116] Ibid., VIII.12.

[117] Ibid.

[118] Ibid., II.4.

[119] Ibid., cf. II.6, II.8.

[120] James, *The Varities*, p. 143.

[121] Augustine, *Confessions*, I.7.

[122] Ibid., I.10.

[123] Ibid., I.20.

[124] Ibid., II.3.

[125] Ibid., IV.16.

[126] Ibid., V.8.

[127] Ibid.

[128] Ibid., V.10.

[129] Ibid., VI.12.

[130] Ibid., VII.3

[131] Ibid.

[132] Ibid., cf., VII.9.

[133] Ibid., VII.12.

[134] Ibid., VII.16.

[135] Ibid., III.5.

[136] Ibid., III.6.

[137] Ibid., cf. IV.3.

[138] Ibid., V.14.

[139] Brown, *Augustine of Hippo*, p. 87.

[140] Augustine, *Confessions*, VI.12, my emphasis.

[141] Ibid., cf. VII.9; Brown, *Augustine of Hippo*, pp. 88-114.

[142] Augustine, *Confessions*, VII.20.

[143] Ibid.

[144] Ibid., VII.21.

[145] cf. Paula Fredriksen, "Paul and Augustine: Conversion Narratives, Orthodox Traditions, and the Retrospective Self" *Journal of Theological Studies* 37 (1986): 3-34.

[146] Brown, *Augustine of Hippo*, p. 101.

[147] Augustine, *Confessions*, VIII.1.

[148] Beyond the text of the *Confessions* itself, the relevant chapters in Brown's *Augustine of Hippo* provide a good starting point.

[149] Augustine, *Confessions*, VIII.2.

[150] Ibid., VIII.4, my emphasis.

[151] Ibid., VIII.5.

[152] Ibid., cf. VIII.2.

[153] Ibid.

[154] Ibid.

[155] James, *The Varieties*, p. 140.

[156] Augustine, *Confessions*, VIII.7.

[157] Ibid.

[158] Ibid., VIII.8.

[159] Ibid., VIII.11.

[160] Ibid.

[161] Ibid., VIII.12.

[162] Ibid., my emphasis.

[163] Ibid., but following the RSV trans. of Romans 13:13-14.

[164] Ibid.

[165] Kenneth Burke, *The Rhetoric of Religion* (Berkeley: University of California Press, 1970), p. 117.

[166] Cf. Brown, *Augustine of Hippo*, p. 160.

[167] Karl Rahner, "Conversion," in Conn, ed., *Conversion*, pp. 203-211; quoted from p. 204, my emphasis.

[168] Bernard Lonergan, "Dimensions of Conversion," in Conn, *Conversion*, pp. 15-21; quoted from p. 18, my emphasis.

[169] I simply follow the sections and sub-sections in the English translation. See below.

[170] Karl Barth *Church Dogmatics; Volume IV: The Doctrine of Reconciliation*, (Edinburgh: T. & T. Clark,

1958), G.W. Bromiley and T.F. Torrance, eds., p. 499
(Barth, CD, IV/2, p. 499).

[171] Ibid., p. 579.

[172] Ibid., cf. pp. 555, 556, 557.

[173] Ibid., p. 553.

[174] Ibid., p. 558.

[175] Ibid.

[176] Ibid., p. 567.

[177] Ibid., p. 581.

[178] Ibid., p. 583.

[179] Ibid., p. 572.

[180] Barth, CD I/2, p. 299.

[181] Ibid., p. 302.

[182] Ibid., p. 301.

[183] Ibid., p. 326.

[184] Ibid., my emphasis.

[185] Peter L. Berger and Thomas Luckmann, *The Social Construction of Reality: A Treatise in the Sociology of Knowledge* (New York: Doubleday, 1966), p. 158.

[186] Ibid.

[187] Rodney Stark and William Sims Bainbridge, *The Future of Religion: Secularization, Revival, and Cult Formation* (Berkeley: University of California Press, 1985), p. 2.

[188] Ibid., cf. pp. 19-37 for definitions of church, sect, and cult.

[189] Cf. David G. Bromley and Anson D. Shupe, Jr., *"Moonies" in America: Cult, Church, and Crusade* (Beverley Hills: Sage, 1979) for an overview of the Unification Church and its career in the United States.

[190] Proudfoot, *Religious Experience*, pp. 10 f.

[191] Ibid., p. 58.

[192] Ibid., p. 61.

[193] Cf. ibid., p. 82.

[194] Anson D. Shupe, Jr., Roger Spielmann, and Sam Stigall, "Deprogramming: The New Exorcism" in James T. Richardson, ed., *Conversion Careers: In and Out of the New Religions* (Beverley Hills: Sage, 1978) p. 150.

[195] Proudfoot, *Religious Experience*, p. 71.

[196] John Lofland and Rodney Stark, "Becoming a World-Saver: A Theory of Conversion to a Deviant Perspective" *American Sociological Review* 30 (1965): 862-874.

[197] Ibid., p. 862.

[198] Ibid.

[199] Ibid., p. 874.

[200] Cf. Stark and Bainbridge, *Future of Religion*, pp. 394-424.

[201] Richard Quebedeaux and Rodney Sawatsky, eds.,

Evangelical-Unification Dialogue (New York: Rose of Sharon Press, 1979), pp. 7f.

202 Ibid., pp. 8f.

203 Ibid., pp. 9f.

204 Ibid., p. 10.

205 Ibid., p. 11.

206 Ibid.

207 Ibid., pp. 11f.

208 Joseph H. Fichter, ed., *Autobiographies of Conversion* (Lewiston, NY: Edwin Mellen, 1987), p. 167.

209 Ibid., pp. 167-8.

210 Ibid., p. 168.

211 Ibid., p. 169.

212 On the Divine Light Mission see James V. Downton, *Sacred Journeys: The Conversion of Young Americans to the Divine Light Mission* (New York: Columbia University Press, 1979).

213 Fichter, *Autobiographies*, p. 169.

214 Ibid., p. 170.

215 Ibid.

216 Ibid., p. 171.

217 Ibid., p. 172.

218 Ibid., p. 174.

219 Stark and Bainbridge, *Future of Religion*, p. 368.

220 Ibid.

221 Ibid., p. 343.

222 Ibid., p. 325.

223 John Lofland, "Becoming a World-Saver Revisited" in Richardson, ed., *Conversion Careers*, pp. 10f.

224 Ibid., p. 11. Much of the work on conversion to the Unification Church has focused on the "Oakland family," the West Coast branch of the movement. It has gradually become clearer, however, that the conversion practices associated with that group were not shared by all Unificationists.

225 Ibid.

226 Edwards, *Crazy for God*, p. 9.

227 Ibid., p. 13.

228 Ibid., p. 15.

229 Ibid.

230 Ibid., p. 17.

231 Ibid., p. 21.

232 Ibid., p. 28.

233 Ibid.

234 Ibid., p. 40.

235 Ibid., p. 41.

236 Proudfoot, *Religious Experience*, pp. 10f.

237 Ibid., p. 112.

238 Edwards, *Crazy for God*, p. 48.

157

[239] Ibid., p. 71.

[240] Ibid., p. 93.

[241] Ibid., p. 102.

[242] Ibid., p. 107.

[243] Cf. Proudfoot, *Religious Experience*, p. 112.

[244] Edwards, *Crazy for God*, p. 135.

[245] Lofland, "Revisited," p. 22.

[246] Ibid.

[247] Barbara and Betty Underwood, *Hostage to Heaven* (New York: Clarkson N. Potter, 1979), p. 44.

[248] Ibid., p. 38.

[249] Cf. ibid., p. 48.

[250] Cf. ibid., pp. 46f., 99f.

[251] Cf. ibid., pp. 101f.

[252] Cf. ibid., p. 77.

[253] Ibid., p. 214.

[254] Ibid., p. 232.

[255] Ibid.

[256] Proudfoot, *Religious Experience*, p. 70.

[257] Underwoods, *Hostage*, p. 226, my emphasis; cf. Stark and Bainbridge, *Future of Religion* p. 421.

[258] Underwoods, *Hostage*, p. 254.

[259] Ibid., p. x.

[260] Cf. Geertz, "Religion as a Cultural System" in *The Interpretation of Cultures*, pp. 87-125.

[261] Stark and Bainbridge, cf. p. 368.

[262] Ibid., cf. 5.

[263] For a critical review of various attempts to define religion see Hans H. Penner and Edward A. Yonan, "Is a Science of Religion Possible" *Journal of Religion* 52 (1972): 107-133.

[264] Stark and Bainbridge, *Future of Religion*, p. 8.

[265] Cf. ibid., pp. 325, 343.

[266] Ibid., p. 6.

[267] Ibid., p. 5.

[268] Cf. ibid., p. 7.

[269] Ibid., p. 7.

[270] Ibid., p. 12.

[271] Ibid., p. 14.

[272] Ibid., p. 325.

[273] Berger and Luckmann, *Social Construction*, p. 158.

[274] For an overview see David B. Barrett, *Schism and Renewal in Africa: An Analysis of Six Thousand Contemporary Religious Movements* (Nairobi: Oxford University Press, 1968).

[275] Jules-Rosette, *African Apostles*, p. 22, cf. p. 28.

[276] Cf. ibid., p. 30.

[277] Cf. ibid., p. 78.

[278] Cf. ibid., pp. 64-67.

[279] Ibid., p. 80.

[280] Ibid., p. 82.

[281] Ibid., p. 87.

[282] Ibid., pp. 58f.

[283] Ibid., p. 73.

[284] Ibid., p. 58.

[285] Ibid., p. 253.

[286] Cf. Proudfoot, *Religious Experience*, pp. 73, 74, 154.

[287] Jules-Rosette, *African Apostles*, pp. 60f.

[288] Ibid., p. 61.

[289] Ibid.

[290] Ibid., p. 64.

[291] Ibid., p. 87.

[292] Ibid., pp. 87-88.

[293] Ibid., p. 88, my emphasis.

[294] Bennetta Jules-Rosette, "The Conversion Experience: The Apostles of John Maranke" *Journal of Religion in Africa* 7 (1975): 132-164; quoted from p. 156.

[295] Cf. ibid., pp. 157-8.

[296] Proudfoot, *Religious Experience*, p. 219.

[297] Cf. Malcolm X, *Autobiography*, pp. 161-168.

[298] Stark and Bainbridge, *Future of Religion*, p. 3.

[299] Jules-Rosette, *African Apostles*, p. 68.

[300] Ibid., p. 70.

[301] Ibid., p. 71.

[302] Cf. Proudfoot, *Religious Experience*, pp. 214-220.

[303] Jules-Rosette, *African Apostles*, p. 214.

[304] Cf. ibid., pp. 233-242.

[305] Cf. ibid., p. 242.

[306] Ibid.

[307] Robin Horton, "African Conversion," *Africa* 41 (1971) p. 85.

[308] Ibid., p. 86.

[309] Ibid., p. 103.

[310] Ibid., p. 101.

[311] Ibid., p. 102.

[312] Cf. Jules-Rosette, *African Apostles*, pp. 239-240.

[313] Horton, "African Conversion," p. 104.

[314] Ibid.

[315] Ibid., p. 106.

[316] Ibid., p. 94.

[317] Ibid.

[318] Cf. Robin Horton, "Neo-Tyloreanism: Sound Sense or Sinister Prejudice" *Man* 3 (1962): 625-634; esp. p. 632.

[319] Cf. Robin Horton, "A Definition of Religion and its Uses" *Journal of the Royal Anthropological Institute* 90 (1960): 297-326; esp. p. 312.

[320]Robin Horton, "On the Rationality of Conversion, Part I," *Africa* 45 (1975): 221.

[321]Cf. Robin Horton, "On the Rationality of Conversion, Part II," *Africa* 45 (1975): 394.

[322]Horton, "On the Rationality of Conversion, Part I," p. 234.

[323]Horton, "On the Rationality of Conversion, Part II," p. 396.

[324]Proudfoot, *Religious Experience*, p. 6.

[325]Ibid., p. 196.

[326]Ibid., p. 197.

[327]Robin Horton and J. D. Y. Peel, "Conversion and Confusion: A Rejoinder on Christianity in Eastern Nigeria" *Canadian Journal of African Studies* 10 (1976): 481-498; quoted from p. 485.

[328]Humphrey J. Fisher, "Conversion Reconsidered: Some Historical Aspects of Religious Conversion in Black Africa," *Africa* 43 (1973) p. 33.

[329]Ibid., p. 36.

[330]Arthur Darby Nock, *Conversion: The Old and the New in Religion from Alexander the Great to Augustine of Hippo* (Oxford: Oxford University Press, 1933), p. 10.

[331]I Thess. 1:9.

[332]Cf. Nock, *Conversion*, p. 1.

[333]Cf. ibid., vii.

[334]Ibid., p. 2.

[335]Ibid.

[336]Ibid.

[337]Cf. ibid., p. 9.

[338]Ibid., p. 7.

[339]Ibid., pp. 7f.

[340]Ibid., p. 8; cf. James, *The Varieties*, p. 171.

[341]Nock, *Conversion*, p. 9.

[342]For the text and English translation of Lucian's *Wisdom of Nigrinus* I follow the Loeb edition of A. M. Harmon, *Lucian* vol. I (Cambridge: Harvard University Press, 1913).

[343]Ibid., 1.

[344]Ibid.

[345]Cf. ibid., 4.

[346]Ibid.

[347]Ibid., 5.

[348]Ibid., 7.

[349]Ibid.

[350]Cf. Nock, *Conversion*, p. 4.

[351]Lucian, *Nigrinus*, 6.

[352]Ibid., 12-14.

[353]Ibid., 14-16.

[354]Ibid., 17-20.

[355] Ibid., 21-25.

[356] Ibid., 26-28.

[357] Ibid., 29-34.

[358] Ibid., 35.

[359] Cf. Nock, *Conversion*, p. 9; James, *The Varieties*, p. 172.

[360] Lucian, *Nigrinus*, 37.

[361] Ibid., 6.

[362] Ibid., 38.

[363] Ibid., 19.

[364] Ibid., 25.

[365] Ibid., 26.

[366] Ibid., 1.

[367] Ibid., 4.

[368] I follow the English translations of Justin's works in Falls, trans., *Saint Justin Martyr*.

[369] For background on Justin's *Dialogue with Trypho* see J. C. M. van Winden, *An Early Christian Philosopher: Justin Martyr's Dialogue with Trypho Chapters One to Nine* (Leiden: E. J. Brill, 1971).

[370] Justin, *Dialogue with Trypho*, 1.

[371] Ibid., 2.

[372] cf. ibid., 2.

[373] Ibid., 3.

[374] Ibid., 7.

[375] Ibid., 8.

[376] Ibid.

[377] Ibid.

[378] Justin, *I Apology*, 14.

[379] Cf. Nock, *Conversion*, pp. 255-257.

[380] See the classic consideration of the audience for apologetic literature in Victor Tcherikover, "Jewish Apologetic Literature Reconsidered" *Eos* 48 (1956) pp. 169-193; see also the general discussions of Christian apologetic works in W. H. C. Frend, *The Rise of Christianity* (Philadelphia: Fortress, 1984); for a lively account of outsiders' accounts of Christianity see Robert L. Wilken, *The Christians as the Romans Saw Them* (New Haven: Yale University Press, 1984).

[381] In general see Bernard Bamberger, *Proselytism in the Talmudic Period* (New York: KTAV, 1968, rev. ed.) and William G. Braude, *Jewish Proselyting* (Providence, RI: Brown University, 1940).

[382] I follow the English translation of *Joseph and Aseneth* by C. Burchard in James H. Charlesworth ed., *The Old Testament Pseudepigrapha* 2 vols. (Garden City, NY: Doubleday, 1985) 2:177-247.

[383] *Joseph and Aseneth*, 6:1, 3.

[384] Ibid., 8:5.

385 Ibid., 9:1.

386 Ibid., cf. 11:5.

387 Ibid., 12:3-4.

388 Ibid., 15:5.

389 Nock, *Conversion*, p. 150.

390 For the *Golden Ass* I follow the English translation of Jack Lindsay, *Apuleius, The Golden Ass* (Bloomington: Indiana University Press, 1960).

391 For a full commentary on book XI of the *Golden Ass* see J. Gwyn Griffiths, *Apuleius of Madauros, The Isis-Book (Metamorphoses, Book XI)* (Leiden: Brill, 1975).

392 Apuleius, *The Golden Ass*, p. 235.

393 Ibid., p. 238.

394 Ibid., pp. 238f.

395 Ibid., p. 244.

396 Nock, *Conversion*, p. 138.

397 Ibid.

398 Ramsay MacMullen, *Christianizing the Roman Empire: A.D. 100-400* (New Haven: Yale University Press, 1984), p. 4.

399 Ibid.

400 Ibid.

401 Ibid., p. vii.

402 Ibid., p. 1.

403 Ibid., p. 29.

404 Ibid., pp. 72f.

405 Ibid., p. 1.

406 Ibid.

407 Theodoret of Cyrus, *History of the Monks of Syria* as quoted in MacMullen, p. 2.

408 Ibid., p. 5.

409 Ibid.

410 as quoted in MacMullen, p. 3.

411 Ibid., p. 52.

412 Ibid., p. 132, n. 22.

413 Ibid., p. 3.

414 Jonathan. Z. Smith, *Imagining Religion: From Babylon to Jonestown* (Chicago: University of Chicago Press, 1982) p. xi.

415 Cf. James, *The Varieties*, p. 34.

416 John Lofland and Norman Skonovd, "Conversion Motifs," *Journal for the Scientific Study of Religion* 20 (1981): 373-385; esp. p. 374.

417 Ibid.

418 Ibid.

419 Proudfoot, *Religious Experience*, p. 43.

420 As quoted in Shea, *Religious Experiencing*, p. 9.

421 Lofland and Skonovd, "Conversion Motifs," p. 375.

422 Ibid.

423 Ibid., pp. 375-383.

424 Ibid., p. 379.

425 Proudfoot, *Religious Experience*, p. 121.

426 Jules-Rosette, *African Apostles*, p. 61.

427 Lofland, "Becoming a World-Saver Revisited," p. 22.

428 Cf. George A. Lindbeck, *The Nature of Doctrine: Religion and Theology in a Postliberal Age* (Philadelphia: Westminster, 1984), pp. 15-41.

429 Ibid., p. 31.

430 Ibid., p. 33.

431 Ibid.

432 Lofland and Skonovd, "Conversion Motifs," p. 377.

433 Ibid.

434 James, *The Varieties*, p. 42.

435 Cf. ibid., p. 41f.

436 Nock, *Conversion*, p. 9.

437 A relatively random sampling indicates that the category "conversion" is used without explanation in collections of texts, monographs, and articles. See, for example, Clarence H. Hamilton, ed., *Buddhism: A Religion of Infinite Compassion* (Indianapolis: Bobbs-Merrill, 1952), p. 39; Edward Conze, ed., *Buddhist Scriptures* (Baltimore: Penguin, 1959), p. 57; Edward J. Thomas, *The Life of Buddha as Legend and History* (London: Routledge & Kegan Paul, 1927), pp. 51, 81; Andre Bareau, *Recherches sur la biographie du Buddha dan les sutrapitaka et les vinayapitaka anciens: de la quete de l'eveil a la conversion de sariputra et de maudgalyayana* (Paris: Ecole francaise d'extreme-orient, 1963), p. 187, passim; Frank E. Reynolds, "The Many Lives of the Buddha" in Reynolds & Donald Capps, eds., *The Biographical Process: Studies in the History and Psychology of Religion* (The Hague: Mouton, 1976), p. 46.

438 Cf. Reynolds, "Lives," p. 41.

439 Ibid., p. 45.

440 Cf. Nock, *Conversion*, p. 150.

441 Cf. James, *The Varieties*, p. 24.

442 Reynolds, "Lives," p. 45.

443 Cf. Thomas, *Life*, p.51.

444 Cf. ibid., p.81.

445 James, *The Varieties*, p. 24.

446 Cf. Bareau, *Recherches*, p. 187.